ENRICH
YOUR LIFE
The Dale Carnegie Way

ENRICH YOUR LIFE

The Dale Carnegie Way

ARTHUR R. PELL, Ph.D.

Dale Carnegie & Associates, Inc.
Garden City • New York

*TO THE MORE THAN
TWO AND ONE-HALF MILLION MEN AND WOMEN
WHOSE LIVES HAVE BEEN ENRICHED
THROUGH THE DALE CARNEGIE COURSES*

Contents

Preface

An enriched life! What an exciting challenge! But is it attainable? It most assuredly is, as it has proved to be for more than two and one-half million men and women throughout the world!

This book is only a partial record of how, by means of the Dale Carnegie method, people have learned to conquer their fears, to develop self-confidence, to generate enthusiasm, and to improve both their personal relations and those with their fellow workers.

Dale Carnegie graduates reading this book will respond to it as an affirmation of their own experiences and of how it has helped alter their ways of life for the better. For one who is just becoming aware of the Dale Carnegie method, and is perhaps considering joining those who have already done so, reading this book will offer a new way of looking at one's life, with an invitation to become a more positive, assertive, self-confident human being. For both the graduate and the one who is yet-to-be a graduate, the book offers a certain excitement through reliving the descriptions and anecdotes on the one hand, and looking forward to experiencing them on the other.

May I express my appreciation to the sponsors, instructors, administrators and other Carnegie staff members who assisted in gathering the information needed to make this book an accurate portrayal of the Carnegie story.

And may I extend particular thanks to Dorothy Carnegie, J. Oliver Crom, Dr. Paul J. Mackey, Richard D. Morgal, Mike Rothenberger, John Cooper, Dr. L. Gray Burdin and John McGrath and all of the executive and administrative staff of Dale Carnegie & Associates, Inc.

Arthur R. Pell, Ph.D.

April 1979

ENRICH
YOUR LIFE
The Dale Carnegie Way

1

Pointing the Way to Self-Fulfillment

Remember, happiness doesn't depend upon who you are or what you have; it depends solely upon what you think. So start each day by thinking of all the things you have to be thankful for. Your future will depend very largely on the thoughts you think today. So think thoughts of hope and confidence and love and success. —DALE CARNEGIE

Jerry Nelson's hand shook as he pressed the sixth floor button on the elevator panel in the office building at 535 Fifth Avenue in New York City. When the elevator stopped at the sixth floor, Jerry stood stock still; he was unable to move as the door opened, closed, and then continued moving up the shaft. He pressed the "six" again, and when it stopped on its down trip, he forced himself to step out. With great trepidation he walked to the end of the hall toward the sign that read "Dale Carnegie Institute Classroom."

Jerry was experiencing a feeling that more than two million men and women have had in the years since 1912—the uneasy feeling that comes with first enrolling in a Dale Carnegie Course. Like many of his predecessors, he was terribly apprehensive about it.

For many years Jerry had been unable to bring himself to attempt anything new. To approach strangers, or acquaintances, to try to know his fellow workers, or members of his church, or even his neighbors, made him nervous and uneasy. He was stymied in his career because he was afraid to present any ideas to his boss, or to participate in any discussions or conferences among his co-workers. On this specific evening he felt particularly unsure of himself and wondered whether he had made the right decision in enrolling for a Dale Carnegie Course.

He had easily identified himself with the man on the TV commercial who said he had possessed little self-confidence before he took the Dale Carnegie Course—but now, as a graduate, he was able to face problems, set goals and relate well to others. On impulse he phoned the number on the screen. A few days later he had arranged for an appointment with Paula Foster, a representative of the Dale Carnegie Institute of New York City.

Paula discussed his goals and desires with him. She pointed out how the Dale Carnegie Course could help him meet most of them. He had signed up for the training and now was about to start the Course. Paula indicated that class members made brief talks at every session. He hoped he would not have to talk to a roomful of strangers tonight; maybe he could still change his mind. The door to the classroom was closed. He could still turn around and nobody would see him leave.

Suddenly he heard a familiar voice say: "Good evening, Jerry." It was Paula Foster, as she joined him at the classroom door. "Welcome to your first class. Let's go in and join the others."

Twenty or more people, all looking ill at ease, were milling around in the room. Within the next ten minutes about twenty more people joined the group. At 6 P.M. sharp, Tom Hill, the instructor, called the class to order. Jerry and his classmates were asked to sit around in a circle, and introductions among the group followed. In this quiet way a carefully planned and structured program was begun that would change the lives of most of those present.

A little later in the session, Tom Hill asked each person what each expected from the course. Jerry told the class he wanted to gain more self-confidence. Betty Feldman, a bookkeeper, indicated that she wanted to be able to communicate her ideas in an orderly and persuasive manner. She said she recognized that interpersonal relations depended on communicating with others, and if she could express her ideas and thoughts in a clear and positive manner, she would earn the respect of others and be accepted by them. She also felt that the course might help her in her job as well as in her social life.

Pete O'Malley, a claims adjuster in an insurance company, said that he was too pessimistic, and needed to be able to handle day-to-day problems in a more positive way. Bill Slovak, who owns a small air-conditioning service company, feared to make decisions and to take the necessary risks. He said: "I always worry about failure. Most of my decisions are good, but if I fail in any of them, I become panicky. I want to develop the resilience to accept occasional failures and to be able to handle them without blowing up and putting myself out of action until I recover."

Kathy Dumas, a housewife, told the group she envied people who exuded enthusiasm. She said she wanted to be able to show enthusiasm in her life. She said that enthusiasm is contagious, and she knew that if she could become enthusiastic it would spread to her family and her friends.

Wally McCarthy told the group that he was a salesman of automobile parts and had a very good sales record with his company. One of his friends had taken the Dale Carnegie Course and had moved up from third to first in sales. Wally commented that he considered himself a success, but he hoped to become even more successful as a salesman, and eventually, to be a sales manager. That was why he had enrolled in the course, he said.

Jerry, Betty, Pete, Kathy, Wally and the other members of this class are typical of the tens of thousands of persons enrolled in the Dale Carnegie Course throughout the world. They missed something in their lives. They felt that they had deep, untapped resources within themselves and they were looking for a way to utilize these resources. They needed to find this way to help them face up to their day-by-day problems and thereby be able to achieve an enriched life, with more joy and satisfaction.

In 1912 Dale Carnegie started a program which has given these tools to over two million people in more than fifty countries throughout the world—men and women of all races, ages, nationalities, occupations, professions and levels of income—the tools and techniques by means of which they have been able to enrich their lives.

In this book we will examine what Dale Carnegie and his successors have done to help people attain this goal. We will, in a sense, visit the classrooms and observe how the graduates of the various Dale Carnegie courses become so much more effective in their business, social and family relations than they were before they undertook the Dale Carnegie courses.

If some soothsayer had told Dale Carnegie on the night he faced his first class at the 125th Street YMCA in New York City in 1912, that he had started a trend in education that would, directly through his courses, and indirectly through his books, affect the lives of millions of people, he would have been astonished. To Carnegie, this was just a class in public speaking. Only later did he recognize that his teaching methods and the materials he and his students developed in the classes, were to be the foundation of a life-enriching process. At each meeting the class members brought to light the problems and the joys of their lives, their defeats as well as their victories. Through these talks the real value of the Course shifted from just the ability to speak, to changes in their entire life style.

As the courses evolved from year to year, Dale Carnegie systemized and standardized them. When it became too much for him to teach, he trained carefully selected groups of instructors in various cities. Today there are over fifteen hundred men and women throughout the world who are qualified as instructors.

The basic philosophy of all Dale Carnegie courses is that through the development of self-confidence, those taking them will become more effective as individuals and lead more fulsome lives.

The success of this philosophy is attested to by thousands of letters from graduates addressed to the Dale Carnegie international headquarters in Garden City, New York, and to the various sponsors of the Dale Carnegie courses throughout the world.[1] They come from factory workers and housewives, from political figures and corporate executives, from teachers and preachers, from all walks of life throughout the world.

Barry Luxon, a steelworker in Hamilton, Ontario, wrote to K. D. Crone Associates, who present the courses in that area:

"I hated my job. I would shy away from telling people what my job was. I hated to go to work and would often get cramps when my shift came. I blew up at my wife. Life was miserable. During the weeks I took the Course I began to develop a better feeling about myself. The night I received an award for my talk on human relations proved to me that all my hard work to improve myself was not in vain. If I could communicate to the people in the class, most of whom did not really know me, then I could communicate to anyone anywhere. This gave me newfound self-confidence. Now I take one day at a time, one shift at a time. I am developing new interests both at work and at home. I tackle all my problems one at a time eagerly and with confidence that I can handle them."

Dorothy Carnegie, chairman of the board of Dale Car-

[1] Individuals who have been carefully selected and licensed to offer the Dale Carnegie courses are referred to as "sponsors."

negie & Associates, Inc., and the widow of Dale Carnegie, reports that no matter where she travels she meets people who have taken the Course and who stop her to tell how much it meant to them. Recently she received a phone call from a schoolteacher who had been on the verge of resigning when he enrolled in the Course. He told Mrs. Carnegie that his enthusiasm for teaching was renewed by the training he had obtained and wanted to thank her and the entire Carnegie organization for giving him the insight that helped him make this important decision.

Many well-known people are graduates of the Course, and many attribute their success to this program. Louie Welch had been defeated in two successive elections for the office of mayor of the city of Houston. He enrolled in the Dale Carnegie Course in 1963 and at his first session told the class that he wanted to improve by 2½ percent because that was the margin by which his opponent had defeated him in the election. After he completed the course he ran again for the same office and was elected to five successive terms, an unprecedented record in that city. He later became president of the Houston Chamber of Commerce.

John Ralston was football coach at Stanford University when the Course was recommended to him. He says: "After a disastrous first year at Stanford, we were looking for help. Dale Carnegie taught us the advantages of living with positive expectancy. Our entire staff took the Course and put the teachings into practice in our coaching. We noticed an immediate change. That year brought us to the Rose Bowl and we credit a lot of our success to Dale Carnegie." Ralston later moved on to become a professional football coach. He was so impressed with the results of the Carnegie training that he had his entire family take the Course and he later qualified to become an instructor.

Many companies have sent considerable numbers of their people to Dale Carnegie classes or have had classes conducted on their own premises for their employees. Some of these nationally known organizations are the Holiday Inns of America, Johnson and Johnson, Hallmark Cards, Peabody Coal Co., Beech Aircraft Corp., McDonald's and General Motors.

Because of the success of the Dale Carnegie Course in Effective Speaking and Human Relations and the demand of graduates for additional Carnegie training, four other courses are now offered by the Dale Carnegie organization.[2] They are the Dale Carnegie Sales Course, which brings the principles of human relations, communication and selling skills together. Enrollment is limited to people who work in the sales fields and it has become the leading course in sales training. The Dale Carnegie Management Seminar brings the principles of human relations to management. Its basic theme is that management is primarily managing people. It leads the student systematically through the basic steps of effective management. Enrollment is limited to persons who are currently in managerial positions.

The other two courses offered are the Customer Relations Course which teaches the principles of dealing with retail customers, and the Personnel Development Course, which is designed to train people in supervising skills or in jobs that involve the techniques of interpersonal relations. These courses are usually conducted exclusively for employees of specific companies.

The textbooks used in the Dale Carnegie courses have had wide circulation over the years. Carnegie's most famous book, *How to Win Friends and Influence People,* is one of the best selling nonfiction works of all time. Over ten million copies have been sold. His *How to Stop Worrying and Start Liv-*

[2] The Dale Carnegie Course in Effective Speaking and Human Relations is usually referred to as just "the Dale Carnegie Course." In this book we shall refer to it as such and spell "Course" with a capital *C*. When referring to the courses in general, a small *c* will be used.

ing has also been a best seller. These books have given many people the incentive to enrich their lives and have encouraged many others to enroll in the Course.

An Ohio graduate wrote: "I read *How to Win Friends and Influence People* and *How to Stop Worrying and Start Living* but I felt that I wasn't able to translate into action what I had read. I accepted what was written on an intellectual level. It is one thing to be aware of things intellectually and another thing to convert this awareness into action that will change your emotions, your behavior, and the way you relate to others. The Course gave me a new set of ground rules to work with. It helped me to change my outlook on life, to better understand the people I encountered, and to reconstruct my entire frame of reference."

In 1979 the Dale Carnegie organization conducted a survey of 15,032 United States class members and their backgrounds. A look at some of the results of this survey and study revealed the following:

Over 70 percent of the class members were between the ages of twenty-five and forty-nine. Nearly three-quarters were male. Almost all had at least a high school education; 33 percent had some college education; 26 percent were college graduates; and 11 percent had postcollege credits. 28 percent had family incomes of from $15,000 to $25,000 and 52 percent had family incomes of over $25,000 a year.

About 25 percent had managerial positions, 22 percent of them were engaged in sales work, 9 percent were in professional positions and 11 percent had supervisory jobs; 57 percent of the students were taking the courses on the recommendation of their employers and 72 percent of the class members had part or all of their tuition paid by their employers.

When asked why they had enrolled in the courses, a variety of answers was received. Self-improvement was listed by

24 percent of the respondents; 22 percent indicated a desire to increase their self-confidence, 15 percent said they wanted to improve their speaking ability and 15 percent said they wished to know more about human relations.

A similar study in Canada showed no significant differences between the American and Canadian class members.

Did these people find what they were seeking in the Carnegie courses? The best indicator of failure in any educational endeavor is the dropout rate. Dale Carnegie dropouts rarely exceed 14 percent of those taking a course. Much of this percentage relates to problems unconnected with it. Considering that the average dropout rate in business, vocational training and other courses runs from 30 up to 50 percent, this is an unusual program. In the 1979 survey, students expressed their satisfaction with the course as follows: 50 percent called it "excellent" and 40 percent said it was "good."

No small part of the success of the program is due to those people who have made a career of Dale Carnegie, either as full-time administrators and representatives or as part-time instructors. These men and women spend considerable time studying and devising ways to make their efforts more valuable to class members. Instructors—at their own expense and on their own time—attend conferences, refresher training sessions and meetings. Dale Carnegie careerists often think of their work as similar to that of missionary or religious leaders. They refer to their jobs respectfully as "the work" and this is reflected in the results. Gerard Weyne, sponsor for Dale Carnegie in France, was asked how things were going. He answered, "How can it be anything but great—I'm selling happiness."

J. Oliver Crom, president of Dale Carnegie & Associates, Inc., attributes the tremendous growth of the organization to the person-centered attitudes of the staff. "It is this kind of dedication, this kind of purpose and commitment that has led us to the edge of greatness. And with the high caliber of people who comprise the membership of this organization, we will be able to keep right on spreading the benefits of Dale Carnegie training throughout the free world."

The training has made people happier. It has enriched the lives of countless class members. It seems to work with people of all ages. One of the Carnegie public service projects is to offer the Dale Carnegie Course at no cost to members of three youth groups: Junior Achievement, Future Farmers of America and the 4-H Clubs. The young men and women enrolled in these programs have reported that they have improved in school grades, won competitions and were planning their lives with more positive attitudes than they had before. At the other end of the age spectrum, many older persons enroll in the course. When Cyrus B. Powers of Wichita, Kansas, was interviewed on his ninety-fifth birthday by the local paper, he commented that one of the highlights of his life was taking the Dale Carnegie Course *when he was seventy-two.*

Another example of a life that was enriched by the Course is Mrs. Mary Housand of Berrien Springs, Michigan. Mrs. Housand was a recent widow who was having difficulty in adjusting to a different kind of life—a life alone in which she would have to earn her living. She was so nervous when, at the first session, she was asked to give her name, that she burst into tears. However, she persisted, and with the support of her instructor and fellow class members she completed the Course. She then went into real estate sales, a field she never thought she would have enough self-confidence and assertiveness to attempt. Within a few years she was elected to the Southwest Michigan Board of Realtors—the first woman to be so honored. In 1973 and again in 1975 she was chosen Realtor Associate of the Year by the local Board of Realtors. In 1976 she was chosen Realtor Associate of the Year by the Michigan Board of Realtors and later was elected a director of the National Association of Realtors.

Class members have made great sacrifices to take the Course. Some have travelled many miles to attend classes. A group of eighteen class members in Australia chartered a bus to bring them from their small town to a city eighty miles away to attend class. Probably the longest round-trip commuter to his class was C. A. L. Morberg of Lynn Lake, Manitoba, who flew 525 miles from his home to the class in Winnipeg and then flew back after class without ever missing a single session. Over the fourteen weeks he flew 14,700 miles.

Joyce Lemming of Malvern, Pennsylvania, tells how she and her husband spent four days canoeing on the Susquehanna River. She reported: "The last morning we skipped breakfast and broke camp before sunrise. We had three or four hours canoeing before reaching our destination. We had to be home by 6 P.M. That morning we encountered the worst stretch of river of the entire trip. Shallow water caused us to run aground over and over again. We dragged the canoe over the rocky river bed to deeper water, then back in to paddle, constantly maneuvering to avoid rocks. After a while my arms felt like lead extensions and the sun became increasingly hot.

"After what seemed an eternity we docked. I went to retrieve the car. I started up the motor, pulled away from the curb. Thump! THUMP! Oh NO, a flat! I broke the bad news to Frank as he struggled his way up the bank with our equipment. Hurriedly, the tire was changed and the canoe tied to the top of the car. We dashed—if anyone can possibly 'dash' on those narrow mountain roads—back to where our van was parked. We quickly changed the canoe from the car to the van. By now my sunburned legs were stinging and our stomachs were vigorously protesting the lack of breakfast and the prospect of a late lunch.

"2 P.M. We stop at a truck stop for gas, a fast bite to eat and check the flat. The air quickly hissed out of a long hole in the wall of the tire. It had been slit with a knife. Another discovery! Raw egg, cooked by four days of hot sun coated the windshield wiper on the right side . . . and it looks as if it may rain.

"On we drive, up and down long hills, around sharp curves, narrow roads with slow country traffic. I'm tapping my left foot impatiently. Time is running out. Relax, I keep telling myself. It begins to rain. The windshield wiper brings the egg right across my path of vision. The washer only makes it worse. In desperation I signal to Frank in the van to pull over and search for something to clean the windshield. We finally find some tissue and Frank's shaving lotion. We scrub and scrub and clear it up enough to see through.

"At last, interstate highway, then finally home. I dash into the house, undressing as I go. Gad, my hair is a mess and my nose is a blistered red. A ton of red river mud washes down the drain.

"Fifteen minutes later—back into the car! I speed along the back roads to the main highway. Thank goodness, traffic is moving along. Only a little further. Then . . . aren't there any parking spaces? I grab my car keys, my book, glancing at my watch—7:30 P.M. Over fourteen hours on the move, but . . . only thirty minutes late to my Dale Carnegie class."

Over the years there have been many people who were skeptical about the value of any self-improvement course, particularly one which was designed to build something so personal, so intangible as self-confidence. Dale Carnegie overcame their skepticism, as have his successors.

Gary Yanker and Jack White, two law students in New York decided to take a variety of "self-improvement" courses and evaluate them to determine if they gave what they promised. The result was a book, *Improving Yourself,* which described their experiences.[3]

Among the courses taken were some concerning memory improvement, speed reading and personality development. Of all the courses reported on, the Dale Carnegie Course received the most favorable evaluation.

Gary Yanker reported the following after taking the course: "I'm surprised now how easily I answer, 'I'll be glad to!' when asked by my hometown librarian to speak to an auditorium full of high school students. The Carnegie Course has definitely changed my attitude toward speaking in public from despair to desire. I am also much friendlier to others and can smile under difficult circumstances. However, I have not turned into a glad-handing, back-slapping automaton. I still get furious, criticize people and complain—but not as quickly as I used to. Carnegie has slowed down my negative emotional reflexes and increased the positive ones, particularly enthusiasm.

"I was enthusiastic before I attended Carnegie Course sessions but showed it only rarely. Now I can become as enthusiastic as a wild monkey at the drop of a hat. But I don't think I am just a barrel of human relations tricks. I am selective in my application.

"When I look over the Carnegie Course material I see that the underlying thought is the need for communication, exchange and warm feeling between people. Carnegie tries to achieve that communication and warm feeling in a number of ways, and I believe the principles he advocates are sound and worthwhile."[4]

There is no special trick that will help you enrich your life. Life can only be enriched by changes in attitude and the

[3] Gary D. Yanker and Jack White, *Improving Yourself* (New York: Dodd, Mead, 1975).

[4] Ibid. pp. 66–67.

application of a sound philosophy of living, whether it be the philosophy of Socrates, or Moses, or Jesus, or Buddha, or Mohammed. These philosophies, combined with the more recent findings of the behavioral scientists and psychologists, are synthesized in the teachings of Dale Carnegie and the courses given by him and his successors.

Some years ago a recent Carnegie graduate was admonished by his hostess at a party as follows: "Don't use any of your Carnegie tricks to ingratiate yourself with me." This is how Dale Carnegie would have answered that remark: "Madam, there are no gimmicks in handling human relations. It is not a bag of tricks—it is a way of life."

Later in this book we will examine this way of life. We will look at Dale Carnegie—the man—and we will see how his work set the stage for changing the way of life of so many people. We will examine the methods used, the experiences of class members, and the techniques we can use to change our own attitudes and thus achieve self-fulfillment and enrichment.

2

Dale Carnegie—The Man

*This is the only chance you will ever have on this earth with
this exciting adventure called Life. So why not plan it, and try
to live it as richly and as happily as possible.*

—DALE CARNEGIE

Who was Dale Carnegie? Who was this man whose work has not only influenced the lives of millions of people all over the world, but whose concepts of teaching have revolutionized adult education methods?

Dale Carnegie was a simple man, a farm boy who never forgot his beginnings even though he achieved success and fame that made his name a household word.

His childhood was no different from other boys brought up on midwestern farms. He helped with the chores, milked the cows and never thought twice about his poverty—perhaps because he didn't realize that his family was poor. He worked side by side with his father in the backbreaking labor of those preagricultural machinery days. A year's hard labor might be washed away by a flood, or seared by the sun, or be destroyed by locusts. Watching how this unceasing toil broke his father's spirit, Dale vowed that he would not spend his life gambling with the weather and crops. Perhaps the chief difference between his childhood and that of other Missouri farm boys was the strong influence of his mother. She was a religious woman who had been a schoolteacher before she married James Carnagey.[1] She encouraged Dale to get an education. Her dream was for him to become a minister or a schoolteacher.

After graduating from high school he entered State Teacher's College in Warrensburg, Missouri. He had a full-tuition scholarship but earned the extra money he needed by working at various tasks. His objective was to obtain his degree and qualify for a certificate to teach in the schools of his home state.

But Dale Carnegie never became a public school teacher. Late in his senior year he encountered a classmate, Frank Self, who had spent the summer between semesters selling correspondence courses for International Correspondence Schools. When Dale learned that Frank had earned as much as twenty dollars a week plus travelling expenses—more than four times the amount his father earned from his hard work on the farm—Dale resolved to make a career in selling.

As soon as school was over, Dale rushed to Denver where the regional office of International Correspondence Schools was located and was hired as a salesman. He was given two dollars a day to pay for his room and meals, plus a commission on all sales.

His territory was western Nebraska, then consisting of only a few towns separated by wide-open spaces. Dale, who was later to make more salespeople successful than anyone before him, did not consider himself a success in selling correspondence courses. One sale that always amused him was to a telephone lineman in Alliance, Nebraska, who was perched on top of a telephone pole repairing some wire when Dale spotted him. With this captive audience, Dale used all of his persuasive powers and sold him a course in electrical engineering.

[1] Dale changed the spelling of his name many years later when he had his offices in Carnegie Hall and felt it was less confusing to coordinate his name with the name of the famous building.

Despite all of his efforts, the farmers and townspeople of Nebraska didn't find the need to purchase correspondence courses. At this time Dale had another chance encounter that changed the direction of his career. Discouraged by his lack of success he expressed his concern to another travelling salesman, a representative of the National Biscuit Company.

This seasoned salesman gave Dale this advice: "Why don't you get a job selling something for which there is a constant demand? I sell crackers and cookies to grocers and general stores. I know every merchant in my territory. I never try to sell them anything. I look over their stock and note what they will need on my next trip. They welcome me and look forward to my monthly visits."

Dale knew one industry that fit this description and with which he had some familiarity—the meat and meat products field. He had helped his father raise cattle and hogs and knew something about meat markets. To get such a job he had to go to Omaha, but he didn't have the money to buy a railway ticket. From his experience on the farm he knew that farmers and ranchers shipping livestock on the freight trains always had to have an extra hand or two to go along. Dale went to the local stockyards and found a rancher who was shipping horses to Omaha. Dale was taken on to feed and water the animals on the 500-mile trip.

In Omaha he was hired by Armour and Company as a salesman. After a month-long training he was assigned the territory of the Dakotas and was given a salary of $17.31 a week plus expenses.

Dale wrote to his parents telling them the good news. His father, who had never been anything but a farmer constantly struggling to make ends meet wrote him a letter: "$17.31 a week!" he commented, "I don't think Armour and Company can keep it up."

Lowell Thomas, in his introduction to *How to Win Friends*

and Influence People, summarized Dale's career with Armour:

"His territory was up among the Bad Lands and cow and Indian country of western South Dakota. He covered his territory by freight train and on stagecoach and on horseback and slept in pioneer hotels where the only partition between the rooms was a sheet of muslin. He studied books on salesmanship, rode bucking broncos, played poker, and learned how to collect money. When an inland storekeeper couldn't pay cash for the bacon and hams he had ordered, Dale Carnegie would take a dozen pairs of shoes off his shelf, sell the shoes to the railroad men and forward the receipts to Armour and Company.

"He would often ride a freight train a hundred miles a day. When the train stopped to unload freight, he would dash uptown, see three or four merchants, get his orders; and when the whistle blew he would dash down the street again lickety-split and swing onto the train while it was still moving."

Despite his success in building up from twenty-fifth to first in sales in his region, he refused a promotion to a management position and decided to take the money he had saved and go to Boston to study to be an actor.

Again a fortuitous meeting changed Dale's plans. Riding on a train in South Dakota, Dale sat next to a Reverend Russell. Russell had formerly lived in New York City and had taught dramatics and produced some plays. When Dale expressed his plan to go to Boston to study speech and drama, the pastor counseled that if he wanted a real basic training in those areas, the place to go was not Boston, but New York City, the center of the theater world. There was a school in New York called the American Academy of Dramatic Arts, which he recommended as the finest training school for actors in the country. Dale accepted his advice and changed his destination—and his destiny.

Upon arriving in New York, Dale went immediately to the

Academy and had an interview with its director, Franklin H. Sargent. In later years he often talked of his "audition." Sargent looked him over and without any other comment commanded him to imitate a chair. Dutifully, he bent his knees and raised his arms to emulate the arms of a chair. With that—and the payment of $400 tuition—he was accepted as a student.

Dale's only role as an actor was with a road company in a play called *Polly of the Circus.* After touring the country with this play for a year, Carnegie decided that there was no future in the theater for him.

When he returned to New York he accepted a job selling cars and trucks for the Packard Motor Car Company. Although he made some sales, he did not enjoy this work. He knew nothing of engines and mechanics and cared less. He felt frustrated and saw little chance of developing a meaningful future for himself.

Years later in a speech before some two thousand listeners in New York City, Carnegie recalled his frustrations and thoughts at that time. "That was the autumn of 1912," he told the audience. "I was twenty-three years old. I said, 'Dale, my boy, is this life? Is this the thing you dreamed about back in college? Remember the grand things you were going to accomplish. You were going to read books. You were going to have time to write books.

" 'And what are you doing? You're coming home every night with a sick headache because you despise the job that you are in . . . This is the turning point of my life! I don't want to make money, but I want to live—that's more important than making money.' "

He made his decision. He would use his days to write and would earn his living—until he could sell his writings—by teaching in a night school. "But what subjects could I teach?," he asked himself. "As I looked back and evaluated my own college education, I saw that the training and expe-

rience I had had in public speaking had been of more practical value to me in business—and in life—than everything
else I had studied in college. Why? Because it had wiped out
my timidity and lack of self-confidence and given me the
courage and assurance to deal with people. It had also made
clear that leadership usually gravitates to the man who can
get up and say what he thinks."

After several rejections by local colleges, Dale decided to
explore the possibilities of giving his public speaking course
at the YMCA. He purposely chose the smallest "Y" in the
city—the 125th Street branch—because he felt they would be
more likely to give him a hearing. The manager was unen-
thusiastic about a public speaking course for businessmen.
They had conducted one at a previous time and it was not
very successful. But the manager invited him to attend a
"social evening" and if he desired, he could make a speech
or entertain.

In those days one of the popular types of entertainment
was the recitation of poems or dramatic pieces. Dale chose
two well-known poems to recite to the group. He prepared
them well using all the expertise developed in college and at
the American Academy of Dramatic Arts. The audience applauded enthusiastically. The manager was so impressed
that he changed his mind about the public speaking classes.
However, he did not want to risk the two dollars a night he
usually paid his teachers. Carnegie agreed to accept 80 percent of the tuition fee, which was paid at each session by the
students.

Dale later recalled: "I had to show concrete results and
show them quickly. What a challenge that was! Those adults
didn't come to my classes because they wanted college credit
or social prestige. They came for one reason only: they
wanted to solve their problems. They wanted to be able to
stand up on their feet and say a few words at a business

meeting without fainting from fright. Salesmen wanted to be able to call on tough customers without having to walk around the block three times to get up courage. They wanted to develop poise and self-confidence. They wanted to get ahead in business. They wanted to have more money for their families. And since they were paying their tuition on an installment basis—and they stopped paying if they didn't get results—and since I was being paid, not a salary, but a percentage of profits, I had to be practical if I wanted to eat."

As in every public speaking course Dale had ever taken, he started by discussing the history of oratory and some of the theories behind good elocution. After only a brief time, he noted two significant things: first, he had told the group as much as he wanted to about oratory and second, the class members looked restless and bored. Something had to be done quickly.

Dale stopped his lecture and calmly pointed to a man in the back row and asked him to stand up. "Give us a brief impromptu talk," Carnegie told him.

"Talk? What can I talk about?"

Carnegie hesitated a moment. "Talk about yourself. Tell us something about your background, your life."

When this student finished, Dale asked another student to speak about himself, and so on until everybody in the class had given a brief talk. "Without knowing what I was doing," Carnegie later reported, "I stumbled on the best method of conquering fear."

Carnegie's approach to teaching through action and participation has since been accepted as one of the most effective ways of obtaining student interest and assuring student attendance. But at that time there were no precedents and no bench marks against which to measure his ideas. However, they caught on and the results have been evident in better speakers and more confident human beings throughout the world.

One incident in those early classes provides a clear example of the value of teaching by personal involvement, rather than by lecture. One of the students in his class was a retired admiral, who couldn't seem to bring any life or excitement into his talks.

"What can I do," Dale asked himself, "to reach this man and draw him out of the invisible shell he seems to have built around himself?"

Another person in the class happened to be a long-haired, wild-talking radical. Just before the next class Dale had a quiet discussion with this young man and explained to him that he wanted to do something to arouse this inarticulate admiral into some kind of action. Would he be willing to make a really strong, anti-American talk that evening? The young radical willingly agreed to go along with this ruse.

He did a better job than Dale could have hoped for. Wide-eyed, wild-haired, he rushed to the front of the room and denounced the government, raved about the evils of the capitalist system and called on the group to rise up and march on Washington.

The admiral, full of patriotic outrage, forgot his fear of facing an audience and came forward. He began to speak, and with deep emotion, expressed his love of his country and its institutions. He hardly realized that he was delivering a talk. The fire in his words was his own expression of his faith.

What was happening here was the spontaneous evolution of a new idea—a new outreach in which Dale and his students together were participating.

The Carnegie concept of teaching public speaking caught on. Within a few months he was teaching classes in YMCAs all over the East Coast. He worked almost every night making as much as thirty to forty dollars a night in commissions. He also frequently asked to give lectures in Carnegie Hall.

In 1916 Carnegie met Lowell Thomas, then a young instructor at Princeton. They became lifelong friends. This friendship later was the cause of a brief hiatus in Carnegie's teaching career. Soon after the end of World War I, Thomas prepared a series of lectures on his experiences as a war reporter with Lawrence in Arabia and Allenby in Palestine. He asked Dale to be his manager. Between them they planned a dynamic program which included a series of slides with comments and anecdotes told by Lowell Thomas. It was so successful that it was presented to sold-out houses for months in London. Dale and Lowell decided to divide the program into two companies, one headed by each, and they toured the United States, Great Britain and Canada for two years.

However, Carnegie's real love was teaching and in 1922 he resumed his classes. Instead of working through the YMCA, he went into business for himself. The real beginnings of the Dale Carnegie organization were now under way.

During one of his visits in Europe, Carnegie met and later married Lolita Baucaire, a woman from the French-German border area. The marriage ended in divorce ten years later. Although Carnegie never discussed his marriage or personal affairs in his talks, this divorce occasionally would be brought up by a heckler.

At one meeting a young woman accosted Dale with: "Mr. Carnegie, do you have a few simple rules for a successful marriage?"

He responded that he had written some articles giving guidelines in that field.

"But," persisted the woman, "Haven't you been divorced yourself?"

"Yes," Carnegie replied, "I have."

"Well, how can you talk about the rules for a happy marriage when you are divorced and obviously were not happy yourself?"

"Madame," Carnegie responded, "who knows more of the pitfalls of marriage and what should be avoided than I?"

During the next twenty years, the Carnegie organization grew into a nationwide network. First business schools were licensed to teach the Dale Carnegie Course; later, special sponsorships were established for the courses. With these beginnings the Carnegie principles spread throughout the United States and across the borders and oceans to the rest of the world.

During this period, Carnegie wrote countless articles that appeared in magazines and newspapers, conducted his own radio programs, in which he interviewed many famous people and told little-known-facts about well-known people. He wrote a number of books, most of which are still read and have been translated into many languages.

His first successful book (earlier attempts at writing had failed—but Dale did not give up) was *Lincoln the Unknown,* a story about the great president which gave the readers much insight into the real Abraham Lincoln. His other books include: *Public Speaking: A Practical Course for Business Men* (1926), which was revised in 1931 and published under the title, *Public Speaking and Influencing Men in Business.* A book based on his radio series, *Little Known Facts About Well-Known People* appeared in 1943. His most famous book, *How to Win Friends and Influence People,* came out in 1936 and *How to Stop Worrying and Start Living* was published in 1948.

How to Win Friends and Influence People won international fame for Dale Carnegie. Both the title of the book and Carnegie's name are known to people in every country in the world. It has been translated into thirty-six languages and published in eighteen countries. Over ten million copies have been sold in addition to the ninety to one hundred thousand copies given to people who enroll in Carnegie classes each year. This book still has a public sale of about ten thousand copies a year—forty years after it was first published.

Its influence is worldwide. When the premier of Burma, U Nu, visited the United States some years ago, he said that as a result of having read *How to Win Friends and Influence People,* the man he most wanted to meet in the United States was Dale Carnegie. Unfortunately, Mr. Carnegie had died before Nu's visit. Nu stated that he had translated for publication in Burma two books: *How to Win Friends* and Karl Marx's *Das Kapital.* Asked which of the two works was the most popular in Burma, Nu replied that "Of course Dale Carnegie outsold Karl Marx." Even the Communist countries have adapted some of Carnegie's ideas. In a recent article in the *New York Times* it was reported that the Russian leaders were instituting programs for better interpersonal relations and were using as a significant resource the materials published by Dale Carnegie.

How to Win Friends was not consciously planned as a public book. It evolved from the material used by Carnegie in his Course. He described its genesis in a talk he gave the year it came out, 1936. He realized, he told his audience that students would come to him only if "you can give them precisely what they want—when you give them something they can use tomorrow to increase their income, to increase their effectiveness in their business and social contacts.

"So I had to be practical. I went over to the public library and to my astonishment I couldn't find a single book on the subject. But I read a lot of magazine articles. Finally I hired a trained research man. He spent eight hours a day for eighteen solid months plowing through countless thousands of magazine articles—reading everything that had the remotest bearing on the subject of how to win friends and influence people.

"Finally, I said to him: 'I'll tell you what I want you to do. I want you to read the biographies of the great men of all ages. I am determined to spare no time, expense, or money to discover how the great men of all ages were able to win friends and influence people. I remember he read twenty biographies of Theodore Roosevelt alone. He read the biographies of everybody from Thomas Edison to Cleopatra. . . .'

"Well, I'd come to the classes and I'd say to the businessmen and women: 'Here's what Theodore Roosevelt did; and this is what Benjamin Franklin did; this is what Lincoln said—Socrates, Plato.

" 'Suppose you go out and try this in your everyday business and social contacts. Try it on your customers, employers and family, and come back a week from tonight and talk about what the results were!' Well, you ought to have seen the enthusiasm. They came to class with something they wanted to talk about because they had had experiences that were stirring within them. And they got up and forgot all about the fact that they were making a speech, and so did the other students.

"Then, of course, we began to discuss it. . . . So you see I have been working in a human laboratory—a laboratory of human relations almost every night in the year for twenty-five years. And the funny part of it is, so far as I know, it is the only laboratory in human relations the world has ever known. I didn't organize it because of my brilliance. We just organized it because it seemed to be the natural thing to do. We never even thought about what we were doing."

As the emphasis of the Course began to shift from public speaking to human relations, using the former as a means to the latter, Carnegie combined the materials developed by his research with the principles brought out in student talks. He decided to publish the result in a private text for his classes, not for the use of the general public.

At that time Leon Shimkin, who was enrolled in his class in Larchmont, New York, entered the picture. Shimkin was a junior executive at the then relatively new publishing firm in New York, Simon and Schuster. (He later became chairman of the board of this company.) He was so impressed by the course and the material used by Carnegie that he persuaded him to allow Simon and Schuster to publish the book.

At the time the book came out, it was considered primarily for the so-called "man in the street." It wasn't realized then that people of all ages and all walks of life and occupations had trouble adjusting to life and getting along with other people. Shortly after the book came out, a two-year survey by the University of Chicago, the American Association for Adult Education and the United YMCA Schools revealed facts that supported Carnegie's beliefs, namely, that people were interested first in their health, and second, in the social skills for getting along and influencing other people.

Carnegie never expected the book to have a big sale. He looked at it primarily as a textbook for his classes. He indicated he would be suprised if it sold five thousand copies.

The book was released in October 1936 with a printing of five thousand copies selling for $1.98 a copy. In the beginning it was virtually ignored by both critics and the public, although a direct mail campaign by the publisher—primarily to business executives—brought an excellent response. About December, it started to pick up in sales. Soon it was selling at the rate of five thousand copies a day. It continued to sell at this rate for about two years. Former students purchased copies for themselves and their friends and relatives. Companies bought hundreds of copies, distributing them among their employees. The book soared to new sales records; within a year more than one-half million copies had been sold—a record for a nonfiction book at that time.

Carnegie was vacationing in Europe when the book started to mount in sales. In a series of frenzied letters and wires he was advised of what was happening. Ecstatic, he returned home. Overnight he was world famous. Within six months he had made $125,000 and was in demand for lectures, radio programs and magazine articles. His first royalty check from Simon and Schuster was for $90,000. His secretary, Mrs. Abigail Connell, recalled that he kept it in his desk for several days, uncertain what to do with it.

Sales continued for years. It continues to sell in hardcover and paperback and is given to students by their parents, to salespeople by their managers and even to constituents by politicians. Some congressmen made a practice of giving copies to every young man and woman graduating from high school in their districts as a guide to living a happier and more successful life. Publications on self-improvement and success motivation still include the book on their lists of recommended readings. Lecturers, clergymen and business executives continue to refer to this book in their speeches.

Examples, illustrations and principles from *How to Win Friends and Influence People* have been quoted by world leaders, business executives and the general public, who very often aren't even aware that their source is the book. Dale would have liked that, because he believed that while his work was not original, it was a synthesis of the thoughts of the great philosophers of all time.

The book made him and his ideas world famous. Paul Sanche, who sponsors the courses in Mexico, reports that even in remote villages in that country, the name of Dale Carnegie is known and respected.

Pope John Paul I quoted Dale Carnegie in the first public audience of his brief reign. He recalled Carnegie's description of a housewife whose husband and children never thanked her for her cooking and housework. Finally, the tired wife put straw on their dinner plates to make them notice her efforts. "It's not always the big favors that make the difference, but the small ones," the Pope said.

In 1944 Carnegie married Dorothy Price Vanderpool. He met her after a lecture he had given in Tulsa, Oklahoma, her hometown. The future Mrs. Carnegie had taken the course in Tulsa and was a friend of the sponsor, H. Everett Pope. After the lecture Carnegie joined Pope and Dorothy for coffee. Upon returning to New York, Dale and Dorothy corresponded for several months. In early 1944 Dale invited Dorothy to come to New York to work as his secretary.

After a somewhat tempestuous courtship, in which Dorothy once quit her job after a spat with Carnegie and started to pack and go home, only to have him turn on the how-to-win-friends charm and influenced her into staying. They were married on November 5, 1944.

The new Mrs. Carnegie discovered hidden talents within herself. She accompanied her husband on his many trips throughout the country and took over many administrative functions in the company. She helped in the development of the courses and wrote her first book in 1953, *How to Help Your Husband Get Ahead in His Social and Business Life,* which has been translated into twenty languages. In 1958 she wrote another successful book, *Don't Grow Old—Grow Up!*

The Carnegie's only child Donna Dale, was born in 1951. Dale was naturally delighted and became a doting father.

Some people who came to hear Dale Carnegie speak may have expected a dynamic, overpowering orator. They may have been disappointed at first as he was an unpretentious speaker. His approach was person-to-person. Yet he was, at the same time, a man of emphatic force on the platform. He could wring his hands to make a point, or pound the table with a closed fist. These were not studied gestures but came out of the man as naturally as his words. He spoke in an impromptu manner, in some instances using notes, in others using no notes at all. His favorite technique was printing large cue words on oaktag pieces or the backs of diplomas and certificates to which he would refer. He used them chiefly to keep on track and to avoid digression from his major theme. Just as he did in his books, he used pointed illustrations to enrich his message. His words flowed from one point to the next, from one meaning to the next, to the final summation.

In his personal dealings he was a plain, down-to-earth human being. He never quite lost the common touch generally associated with farm people. In an article in *Success Unlimited,* Bill Stover, long-time associate of Dale Carnegie, wrote: "Actually he was shy, often self-conscious, more likely to mark himself down than up. He was very emotional, dramatically inclined, easily persuaded, very changeable, much too soft-hearted and trusting for his own good. Once you got to know him he was warm, friendly, and loyal to a fault. He was a man of integrity with strong convictions, abundant energy and contagious enthusiasm. He was truly humble."[2]

Harold Abbott, his long-time friend and travelling companion, once said, "Dale Carnegie is a man of great ability, yet of greater humility. Despite being a such sought-after celebrity, he never considered himself great. He refused most social invitations because he said: 'People expect me to be something out of this world. But when strangers meet me they find I'm just like their next door neighbor—that I'm not someone with a dynamic personality. Then they feel let down. I sense that feeling, and I'm embarrassed.' So he just asked to be excused."

Paul Werner, who was a neighbor of the Carnegies in Forest Hills and is now a Dale Carnegie sponsor in England, concurs in this evaluation of Carnegie's personality. "He had no pretensions," Werner recalls. "He was very sensitive toward people. He identified with the average man and could speak to anyone at their own level. He never made you feel he was an important person."

[2] W. H. M. [Bill] Stover, "Dale Carnegie: The Man Behind the Legend," *Success Unlimited* 23, no. 4 (Chicago: April 1976).

Werner tells of a time when his wife Jane was raising poodles. Dale and Dorothy were visiting them and after a while Dale disappeared. They found him playing with the Werner children and the puppies. He was as absorbed in the children's conversation as he would be in conversation with adults.

Norman Vincent Peale, whose work as a minister, author and lecturer paralleled Carnegie's and who was an admirer and friend of his, chose Carnegie to be the first layman to preach a sermon at his Marble Collegiate Church. Carnegie told about his early childhood and recalled that there were times when there was practically no food in the house, but that never bothered his mother. She would always say, "Don't you worry. The Lord will provide. We love the Lord and He loves us. He's not going to let us starve." When he got to talking about this, all of a sudden, he stopped. There was dead silence. I was sitting there by him and I could see that he was all choked up. He was really overcome—and it was a long minute or two before he could continue. His sermon was really a kind of a personal expression as to his religious faith. It was absolutely beautiful."

Dale Carnegie's teachings have influenced people in all walks of life and in many countries. Dr. Pratap Pendse, now a professor of biological sciences at California Polytechnic University, read *How to Win Friends and Influence People* when he was a fourteen-year-old in India. He wrote to Mr. Carnegie and told him how impressed he was and asked him to send him a rule to live by. Dale Carnegie wrote back and sent him this advice: "Whenever you see a thistle, pull it up and plant a flower." Dr. Pendse still has this message and it is one of his proudest possessions. His whole life has been permeated with the Carnegie philosophy and he encourages his students at the University to study Carnegie's writings and take the Course.

Bernard Meltzer, a businessman who worked himself up

from poverty to become a millionaire and then changed careers to become a very popular commentator and adviser on a New York radio station, was the subject of a profile in the *New Yorker* magazine. In discussing the influences on his life, he said "The one book which really turned my life around was *How to Win Friends and Influence People* by Dale Carnegie. I read it a hundred and ten times. I committed it to memory. I tried to practice a chapter a day. It *worked,* by the way."[3]

Bill Stover tells that Carnegie, like most gifted people, was a man of moods. He had a temper, but was quick to reverse himself and would try to make amends if he broke one of his own rules.

"If you're wrong, admit it quickly and emphatically," was a cardinal Carnegie rule. And he took his own medicine. He told me once, 'Bill, I try not to make too many mistakes, but when I make one it usually is a beaut. If the blooper is in writing, I file it away on the top of my desk in my Darn Fool Mistake file. Then when I start getting too swell-headed, I reach for my DFM file and read aloud some of my asinine mistakes until I come back to earth."[4]

Stover reported that Carnegie's most outstanding characteristic and perhaps the real secret of his success was his highly contagious enthusiasm about everything he did. "He'd bubble over with such excitement over an idea that others would find themselves carried along in the current of his spontaneous emotion."

Dale Carnegie died on November 1, 1955, a few weeks before his sixty-seventh birthday. The funeral services were held in Forest Hills, but he was buried in Missouri near his parents.

[3] James Stevenson, "Profile—Bernard Meltzer," *The New Yorker* (August 14, 1978), p. 39.
[4] Stover, op. cit.

On November 3, 1955, the following obituary appeared in a Washington newspaper:

Cynics used to speculate about what life would be like if everybody absorbed and practiced the teachings of Dale Carnegie. Mr. Carnegie, who died Tuesday, never worried about the wisecracks of the sophisticated. He knew what he was doing, and he did it remarkably well. In his books and his classes, he sought to teach the average man how to overcome his feelings of inadequacy—how to speak—and as his most famous book put it, how to win friends and influence people.

Literally millions were influenced by his common sense philosophy, as old as civilization and as simple as the commandments, but a valuable aid to happiness and achievement in these hectic times.

Dale Carnegie solved none of the profound mysteries of the universe. But, perhaps, more than anyone of his generation, he helped human beings learn how to get along together—which seems sometimes to be the greatest need of all.[5]

[5] Ibid.

3

Acquiring Self-Confidence

If you want to develop courage, do the thing you fear to do and keep on doing it until you get a record of successful experience behind you. That is the quickest and surest way ever yet discovered to conquer fear. —DALE CARNEGIE

Leo Callahan, new chief of police in Fort Lauderdale, Florida, was very brave in his job as police officer, but he was terrified when he had to speak to a group of people. Callahan had apprehended criminals at gunpoint on numerous occasions, but as he put it, "getting up before more than one person was a gut-turner." After taking the Dale Carnegie Course, Callahan gained the confidence to make those public talks and he attributes this to be a significant contributor to his promotion through the ranks and eventually to chief.

The development of self-confidence is the key factor in Dale Carnegie training. Most of the participants in the Course report that although they obtain other benefits as well, the growth of their self-confidence was the major benefit derived from their experience.

How does the Carnegie method accomplish this? By requiring all the class members to speak at least once in every class to an appreciative and encouraging audience, participants develop the confidence needed to overcome their fears.

Dale Carnegie counseled his instructors to regard the Course as a means of destroying fear and building self-confidence. He said: "Think of it as a course in human relations. Think of it as a new way of life. For it often is just that. When a person banishes fear and develops confidence, his ceilings will become higher and his vision unlimited."

Carnegie recognized that often beginners would be more likely to feel encouraged and inspired by the testimony of graduates than by lectures given by instructors. He recommended that recent graduates be invited to appear before beginners' classes to tell how they overcame their fears and how delighted they are at the opportunity now given them to relate their experiences. He also recommended that they tell what increased confidence has meant to them in terms of physical and mental well-being and how it has helped them in their work and in their personal lives.

Carnegie cautioned his instructors to keep in mind that their responsibility is . . . *"to conquer fear and develop poise, courage, and self-confidence."* "We have found" he said, "that the surest, quickest way to help a person gain courage and self-confidence in everyday life is by developing courage and self-confidence in speaking before groups.

Since we would only increase—not destroy—a person's self-consciousness and fears by criticizing that person's accent, grammar, voice or gestures, we do not criticize those features of a talk during the first part of the Course. You can help a person develop courage and confidence only by giving him or her a sense of accomplishment and victory."

Mary Willis, who took the Course in New York City, was blind, and she came to class with her German shepherd seeing-eye dog. For the first few sessions Mary was afraid to go to the front of the room to give a talk. Her instructor and classmates went out of the way to encourage and help her overcome this fear. After a few weeks, Mary became less reluctant to step forward and speak. Soon she complained that the class was being over-protective; she said she wanted to be treated like everyone else. After some weeks Mary missed a session, which she made up by attending a different class. With no hesitation or fear or qualms, she gave an excellent talk before the new group. In her graduation talk, she stressed the fact that she had acquired enough confidence to leave her job and seek one which would give her more money and job satisfaction. Her classmates responded by writing a glowing letter of recommendation to potential employers.

It is this feeling of courage that is the basis of the entire Dale Carnegie program and that motivates every class. Carnegie quoted military leaders, famous movie stars, singers, and noted political leaders, who admitted that they had lacked courage at different times in their lives, and told how they overcame their fears and had been able to face up to difficulties.

In a speech before the Association of Commerce in Milwaukee a few years before he died, Dale Carnegie summed up this concept: "I would rather leave my children a heritage of self-confidence and courage than one million dollars."

"Other than by encouraging talk, in what other ways can a person develop courage?" Carnegie was frequently asked. In a radio talk on this subject he said:

"One thing is sure. You can't buy courage. Real courage can be developed just as you would develop a strong arm. You know that you couldn't go to a physical trainer and buy a strong arm even if you had the wealth of Rockefeller and Henry Ford put together, but you can develop a strong arm by chopping wood or hammering a punching bag; and, in the same way you can develop your courage by using it.

"Begin tomorrow by doing something you fear to do. Emerson said: 'Do the thing you fear to do and the death of fear is absolutely certain.' You can never develop courage by sitting down and doing nothing. You develop courage only by action. Take myself, for example, I am afraid to dive off a springboard six feet high. Why am I afraid? Because I have never done it, but if I forced myself to do it and keep on doing it no matter how awkward I was, until I got a record of successful experience behind me, why, naturally, I would soon have the courage and want to dive off a springboard twenty feet high.

"Suppose you know someone you are afraid to call on. All right, then call on that person tomorrow. Do the thing you are afraid to do. You may be so scared that you have to walk up and down in front of his home or his office half a dozen times before you enter. Once you are in and face the situation you will usually find it is not as bad as you feared."

Dale Carnegie sponsors throughout the world report countless experiences which prove this point. One of the most dramatic was that of Maud Danziger of Cape Town, South Africa. Her story was reported by Robert E. Hopkins, a Carnegie careerist in Cape Town:[1]

"Maud was a housewife who had built such a stout wall between herself and the outside world that for the last five years she had never voluntarily moved out of her house, not even to buy vegetables from the lorry which stopped outside her garden gate. The household shopping which she could not do by telephone her husband had to do for her. On one occasion when painters were at work on the outside of her house she let them do the whole place over in the wrong color rather than go out to speak to them.

"One evening her husband managed to persuade her to attend a Dale Carnegie demonstration meeting, where she won a door prize. She was called three times before her husband could maneuver her into the aisle to receive it. When she finally came onto the stage she was one of the most frightened looking people I had seen in all my experience.

"Maud enrolled in the Course. She was so terribly nervous

[1] William Longgood, *Talking Your Way to Success,* (New York: Association Press, 1962) pp. 77–79.

that when she got home after the first session, she lay awake all night shaking. By the third session she realized that this Course was the most exciting and exhilarating thing that had ever happened to her. It lifted her completely out of the narrow world she had shaped for herself; suddenly life became a challenge.

"After finishing the Course, Maud worked as a graduate assistant. She was engaged by the South African Broadcasting Corporation for a series of three broadcasts on their 'Woman's Hour' where she told her story. She called it 'The Miracle.' "

No less "miraculous" are the stories of business executives whose lives and careers were expanded through the acquisition of greater confidence. Bill Murray, now retired, was a senior executive in a construction company in Phoenix, Arizona. Bill had no fear about making decisions that involved hundreds of thousands of dollars, but he so feared even reading a letter to a group of people, that his hands shook. For many years he had paid somebody to read a speech he would write for the annual company Christmas party. After taking the Course, Bill not only delivered the speech himself, but became a leading spokesman for his company, and for his industry throughout the country.

Another businessman whose career was changed by the Course was John A. Abom, now president of Analytic Plastics Company of Bristol, Pennsylvania. He said:

"At the time I took the Dale Carnegie Course I was in the plastics department of Rohm and Haas working as an engineer on new molding techniques. Periodically we had groups come in from large companies like Ford and General Motors, who used our products. We would get a group of a dozen people for a three-day training session. I was responsible for arranging the programs and talking about the new molding techniques. I hated it and didn't look forward to it one bit. I had butterflies in my stomach. First I would look at the blackboard, then I would stare at the floor. I would get two words out and the audience seemed to fall asleep on me.

"One of my co-workers suggested I take the Dale Carnegie Course. After a few sessions I began to loosen up. A few weeks later, I couldn't wait to try the new methods I had learned in the Course. If I wanted my audience to be happy, I could make them happy. If I wanted them to be sad, I could make them sad.

"Really, what happened was that I acquired self-confidence that gave me the ability to talk before a group of people I couldn't face before. It was not any trick or technique of speaking that did it, but my own confidence in myself.

"More important, it helped me get out from under my shell and make the transition from engineering to sales, and eventually to opening my own business."

This need to develop greater self-confidence is especially felt by new widows. Often, their entire lives having been centered around their husbands, their plight was even more tragic because of their inability to face the future alone, as independent individuals. The courage and self-sufficiency acquired by speaking before a class and receiving its support, has helped these women to reestablish meaningful lives. One widow, Hazel Lawson of Battle Creek, Michigan, had tried to overcome the shock of her widowhood by travelling. She visited the Holy Land, went to South America, to Africa, India and the USSR, and later made two complete trips around the world. On returning, she was asked to tell about her trips. Mrs. Lawson said: "I am a college graduate and had taken courses in public speaking and expression, but I was scared to death to speak in public. I also knew that just showing slides of my trip without describing the excitement of each place would bore my listeners. The Dale Carnegie Course helped me with both problems."

By means of vivid demonstrations, Mrs. Lawson would illustrate her talks in a most unusual way. "I would dress in native garb; for instance, in describing my trips to South America, I'd dress like an Indian woman with a big bundle (washing) on top of my head and a baby (big doll) on my back, wearing shawls and jewelry. I sometimes carried a blow gun with poison arrows in my hand or a shrunken head."

Her talks were so successful that she became a much-sought-after speaker. In addition, she gained so much self-confidence that it carried over into her ability to manage her late husband's business affairs.

Mrs. Lawson attributed her success to her Dale Carnegie training and wanted to help other people gain confidence. She observed that many young clergymen graduating from seminaries were unsure of themselves in addressing their congregations or other groups. To help these young clergymen Mrs. Lawson arranged to finance their tuition in the Dale Carnegie Course. Graduates of theological seminaries in her area were offered a chance to take the course at her expense, less a small token payment, so as to indicate some personal investment in the course. Twenty-eight young clergymen have taken the training under Mrs. Lawson's auspices. As a direct result of her enthusiasm about the Course, over 150 people have enrolled in it.

Dale Carnegie believed wholeheartedly that fear can be overcome by standing up and speaking before a class. He said:

"No matter what a pathetic failure a person makes—even if so terrified that he or she can only utter half a sentence, that person is to be congratulated because it takes courage to do something that not one person in a thousand has the courage to do—improve the most important person in the world—oneself."

This training is probably the best way yet devised for banishing fear and developing courage and self-confidence. Why? Because, when a person loses the fear of speaking before groups, fear of self, of others and of life itself is overcome. One has an entirely new concept of oneself, and is inspired to undertake and accomplish things never dreamed possible before.

The first step in developing courage is the attitude toward whatever it is one fears. One should keep in mind Marcus Aurelius' maxim: "Our life is what our thoughts make it."

Dale Carnegie and his staff did a great deal of research on the subject of developing courage. They read the lives of great men and women throughout the ages, and Carnegie himself interviewed many famous people who had overcome handicaps to achieve their goals. People like Eddie Rickenbacker, Franklin and Eleanor Roosevelt, Charles Schwab, Marconi, Helen Keller and many other well-known men and women told Dale Carnegie that his views on overcoming problems had given them the strength and perseverance to succeed.

In a radio interview, Vash Young, a man who pulled himself out of obscurity and poverty into riches and fame, told his story to Dale Carnegie. At that time he had become one of the most successful insurance agents in the United States and one of the highest paid salespeople in the world. He was also the author of five books, four of which became best sellers.

Young told of his poverty and lack of education. He described how he had planned to kill himself by jumping out of a hotel window. He said: "I tried to drink enough courage out of a whisky bottle to jump out of the window. Well, I overtrained. I drank so much that I forgot to jump and the next morning I awoke in a more deplorable condition than before."

This experience made Young reexamine his life. He said to himself, "Look here, stupid. Suppose you owned a factory that was intended to make ice cream and you found that it was not manufacturing ice cream but carbolic acid—

wouldn't you do something about it? All right, Vash Young, you have a thought factory. It is inside you. You own that factory. You can boss it. But are you bossing it? The answer is 'No'. I was letting it run wild. My thought factory was manufacturing junk. It was producing worry, fear, envy, anger, self-pity, gloom, unhappiness and poverty. I didn't want junk like that. Nobody would want it.

"From being a self-made enemy, I simply switched over into being a self-made friend. I suddenly realized that by changing my thoughts I could change my life. I followed the biblical statement: 'As a man thinketh in his heart, so is he.' "

It was not an easy battle to win. Young determined to develop nine qualities: love, courage, cheerfulness, activity, compassion, friendliness, generosity, tolerance and justice. He frequently had to fight back the thoughts he did not want. "I did this," he said "by talking out loud against the thoughts I didn't want. I made a game of it. When I discovered thoughts of envy or fear trying to sneak through the door of my consciousness, I would say, 'You go take a jump in the river. You ruined my life in the past—now get out and stay out!' "

If attitude is the foundation of building self-confidence, resolution is the technique that solidifies attitude into a way of life. Dale Carnegie brought this out in his books, his public speeches and private consultations and in his teaching of the courses he developed. "If we *really* want to improve ourselves, we have got to form new habits. Our lives, our characters are just the sum total of our daily habits. Our habits are ourselves. Carnegie frequently spoke of William James' four rules to help form new and desirable habits:

"(1) *Start yourself off with all the enthusiasm at your command.* When it came to forming new habits, no one had anything on old Benjamin Franklin. Early in life Franklin drew up for himself a list of thirteen characteristics he wanted to cultivate. He called them his *thirteen virtues.* He concentrated on one virtue each week, until he had covered all thirteen. Then he went back to the beginning and began all over again. He realized that habit is nothing but repetition—and repetition is nothing but habit.

"Now most of us make good resolutions from time to time but we forget about them. Franklin didn't. He struck while the iron of his enthusiasm was hot. And he kept at it, day in and day out. And by making a game of it, he never let his enthusiasm cool. So our first rule comes from old Benjamin Franklin: when you want to form new habits, start yourself with all the enthusiasm at your command. Make the formation of this new habit seem like the most important achievement in the world to you for the time being. Keep reminding yourself of the desirable things this new habit will mean to you.

"Maybe it will improve your health. Maybe it will increase your popularity, your income or your self-respect. Keep 'selling' yourself on its importance until your enthusiasm reaches the boiling point.

"(2) *Grasp every opportunity for practicing your new resolution.* I knew a man named William Steinhardt. He was a pretty glum individual, but after I talked to him one night about the value of a smile, he decided he was going to learn to smile. He didn't hesitate.

"He started in the very next morning. As he sat down to breakfast, he greeted his wife with a smiling 'good morning, my dear.' She nearly fainted, of course, but he told her that from now on she could expect a smile with breakfast every morning. He smiled at everyone he met that morning: at the elevator man, at the doorman, at his office staff. He smiled at people who had never seen him smile before.

"You see, Bill Steinhardt didn't procrastinate. He went right to work and today he's one of the most congenial men I know.

"(3) *Don't permit yourself to fail even once.* Don't be like Rip

Van Winkle who said, every time he got drunk, 'Well, I won't count it this time,' because as Professor William James said: 'Every lapse is like the letting fall of a ball of string which one is carefully winding up; a single slip undoes more than a great many turns will wind again.'

"Free-lance writers know the value of keeping everlastingly at it. Jack London, for example, made it a rule to write one thousand words a day, day in and day out. Mary Roberts Rinehart told me she writes five hundred words a day, even if it's only in her diary.

"(4) *Burn your bridges behind you.* That's what Julius Caesar did after sailing across the English Channel and landing his army in what is now called England. Well, he didn't burn his bridges, but he did burn his ships behind him. He set fire to the ships that brought his soldiers across the channel and he had his army stand on the Cliffs of Dover and look down on the burning vessels. He told them that here they were in enemy country without any means of retreat and that there was nothing else to do but to advance and conquer. And that's precisely what they did.

"Now, when you and I are trying to form a new habit, let's take a tip from old Julius Caesar and make it impossible for us to retreat.

"For example, the president of a large rubber company in Ohio once telephoned me saying that he wanted to learn to speak in public and that he wanted to enroll in a certain course in New York. But he got cold feet and never did anything about it.

"However, when last autumn rolled around, he did something that made it difficult for him to fail. He told all his friends and associates that he was going to come to New York every Monday night to attend a course in public speaking. That made it impossible for him to back out. He *had* to come to New York then or he would have been laughed at. You see, it was harder for him to break his resolution than it

was for him to keep it. Or in other words, he burned his
bridges behind him . . . made it impossible to retreat."

How are these concepts translated into action in the
classroom? Class members are constantly encouraged by the
comments, applause and awards they receive from their instructors and classmates. This atmosphere of approval does
more to develop self-confidence than lectures, sermons,
reading inspirational literature or private consultations.
Other encouragements stem from awards for reporting, by
evidence of improvement in the application of the principles
of human relations, and by developing self-confidence
through the control of worry.

Mike Evans, who took the course in Chicago because he
wanted to get enough confidence to talk to his boss, used his
newfound courage to show his boss the award he received in
the class. His boss was so proud of him that he borrowed it
and kept it for four weeks to show to others.

Each of the early sessions of the Course is designed to
build up self-confidence among the class members. These
sessions culminate in a very exciting "fun session" where the
speakers are heckled by their fellow class members. By force
of voice and actions, class members stand up to this heckling
and are thus reaffirmed in their self-confidence.

It would be nice to say that every student is brimming with
courage. That is not so, for many need continual reenforce-
ment and encouragement. Each session gives the student
additional self-confidence. It comes from the applause of the
other class members, from the comments of the instructor,
from the awards, and from consultations with the graduate
assistants as well as with the instructor, during the breaks,
before and after class.

As Mrs. Miek Staats of Houston, Texas, said: "When I
moved to Houston I had no friends and I was very lonely. I
felt sorry for myself but did not have the courage to go out
and meet people. The Course gave me self-confidence. I

have made more friends in the last two years (since taking the Course) than I did the first eight years I was in Houston. People come to me now and cry on my shoulder and ask my advice. Only a few years ago I wished I had someone I could go to, and now I'm the one others call on."

Vicki Fisher of Wilmington, North Carolina, gained the self-confidence necessary to present her point of view to her boss when she felt she had been treated unfairly. She reported to her class: "Three years ago during a performance appraisal with my boss, I was asked to set a professional goal. I set my sights on becoming a materials analyst. During the next three years I learned all I could in that department by attending classes and seminars. I thought my opportunity had come when the company was planning to create a new materials analyst position.

"My optimism waned, however, when I found out that the company had started interviewing outside applicants for the job, all men, all college graduates. After some hesitation I approached the boss and asked him if he was considering me for that position. He said he was not planning to interview me because he wanted a strong person in that job, one who could make some changes in the department. I was not satisfied with this reason for disqualifying me. By the time we had finished our talk, I was furious, but I kept my composure and left.

"The more I thought about it, the worse I felt. I had really made an effort toward qualifying for the job and had all but been promised it by the supervisor of the Materials Department. I finally decided that I would talk to my immediate supervisor's manager, the head of our department.

"I explained the situation to him and told him that I felt I had been treated unfairly. I was not a college graduate, but the job did not call for a degree and most of the other materials analysts were not college graduates either. I had studied and worked for this job and was willing to match my background against any of the other candidates. He agreed and said he would ask my boss to grant me an interview.

"The next morning my boss called me into his office. He was very angry, so much so that he was shaking. He berated me for going over his head. But I remained calm, knowing I was right. He would not have been so angry, I think, if his superior had not agreed with me.

"I wish I could conclude this talk by saying that I got the job. However, the company, faced with other problems, decided not to fill the job at that time. But I really felt good inside because, for the first time in my life, I had shown enough self-confidence to stand up for myself. Once my boss cooled down, I noticed that he treated me with a new respect. I think I stand a good chance of getting that job when the opportunity comes up again."

The development of self-confidence is a thread which is woven through all of the five Dale Carnegie courses. It is essential to the Sales Course. If salespeople are not confident in themselves, how can they convince others to buy their products or services? This also applies to the Customer Relations Course.

Norman Sisisky, president of Pepsi-Cola Bottling Company of Petersburg, Virginia, had a number of his people take the Customer Relations Course. He commented:

"The course gave my people confidence—confidence in themselves. It gave them the confidence and the ability to express themselves. Many of these people were route drivers who did not have much education, but by developing this confidence, they were able to do their job more effectively and, more important for us, were able to move into middle-management jobs.

"They developed confidence in themselves and this expressed itself in more confidence in talking to us in management. They were able to communicate to us some of their ideas which were beneficial to the entire enterprise."

Raymond Berry, who held the world's record for receiving passes when he was a player with the Baltimore Colts, took the Dale Carnegie Personnel Development Course when he was the assistant coach of the Detroit Lions football team. When he completed the program he told his instructor: "This course helped me to be more of a thermostat than a thermometer. It has given me the ability to control what is going on inside my heart and head no matter what is going on outside." This is the epitome of self-confidence.

In 1974 the U.S. Marine Corps Recruiting Station in Seattle, Washington, used the Dale Carnegie Sales Course to help their recruiters attract and convince young men and women to join the Marines. Do Marines have to develop self-confidence? Well, Marines may face an enemy with confidence, but convincing others to enlist is quite another matter.

The commander of the unit wrote to Ken Harrison, then Carnegie sponsor in Seattle:

"During April, May and June of 1974 a group of Marines from our recruiting station took the Dale Carnegie Sales Course. . . .

"At the Recruiting Station in Seattle a production average of 4.0 is considered outstanding and a production average of 3.0 is excellent.

"This group was compared with a similar group of recruiters who did not receive the Dale Carnegie Sales training. The average productivity of each group was 2.9 new accessions into the Marine Corps each month at the end of March 1974. At the end of March 1975 the group which had not received the Carnegie training has raised its average to 3.4 accessions per recruiter, per month. The group that did receive the Dale Carnegie Sales training had raised its average to 3.9 accessions per recruiter per month, or only one percentage point short of achieving an outstanding rating. The biggest noticeable difference between the groups is the confidence with which the Dale Carnegie graduates approach their daily jobs when compared with the nongraduates. This confidence combined with a more certain knowledge of how to sell effectively are in my opinion direct results of the training received."

Even more dramatic was the sensational turnaround of an entire city. By applying the Carnegie principles and developing group self-confidence, Poplar Bluff, Missouri, experienced a rebirth.

In the early 1960s this once thriving town of fifteen thousand people in the foothills of the Ozarks was dying. Dying is a word rarely used to describe a town's condition, but this community had just stopped caring about whether it continued to exist or not.

On the surface it appeared to be an average mid-American community. The people were good people—solid, hard-working blue collar and white collar employees, small business owners and managers, salespeople, household heads and professional people. They were a churchgoing community. They counted about forty-four churches of regular denominations and a sprinkling of less traditional churches.

It was a delightful place to live—a good place to raise children. If one loved the outdoors, there was an abundance of opportunity for hunting, camping, boating and fishing in nearby Clark National Forest and Lake Wappapello.

What had gone wrong? A ride around the town would show the symptoms to anyone who would take the time to look. Houses were in disrepair. Many of them were well below the standards for decent living. A good many were the shacks seen so often in rural or semi-rural slums. Driving over some of the roads would shake the car and strain the springs. Outside of the main streets, the roads were unpaved, or where there was a pavement, it was so rutted that it was unsafe. School buildings were old and dilapidated.

Factories had closed and no new industries were coming in because of inadequate housing, poor schools, bad roads and insufficient electric power. The young people were leaving and the prospects for those who remained were discouraging.

The heart of the problem lay with the archaic sewer system. Only 40 percent of the community had sewers. Until this was corrected no new housing, schools or even factories could be built. Yet when the city fathers tried to float a bond issue for more and better sewers, it had failed.

How could those Poplar Bluff citizens who cared about their town change the situation when the majority were so lethargic and complacent? The well-to-do seemed to care little about their less fortunate citizens and many of the disadvantaged townspeople seemed to have no other goals than to survive in their poverty.

Over a period of some years this defeatist attitude deepened into the community consciousness and became a way of life. In the better areas of town the people kept their neighborhoods in reasonably good condition, while "on the other side of the tracks" the neighborhoods deteriorated steadily.

But there were some people in this city who felt there must be some way to reverse the situation. Could this lost community be brought back to the self-respect it once enjoyed? Could the people living here once more find new meaning in their lives, some motivation to halt the decay and rebuild the town?

Groups met here and there around town for discussions, and meetings were held at various places. Parents, unable to keep their grown children in town, discussed the lack of opportunities with other parents and wrung their hands in despair. Service groups talked about nothing else at their meetings. Someone had to do something about it, but who was knowledgeable, and capable and willing enough to undertake such a project?

A slight feeling of hope began to develop in Poplar Bluff. People of all strata of the community talked of nothing else. At the supermarkets the shoppers exchanged ideas; at the pharmacy, the bowling alley, the barber shop, talk centered on solving this problem. But how and who?

As in so many similar situations, it was finally recognized that the only people who could keep this town from dying were the people themselves.

This was their critical decision, their moment of truth. It was their problem, and therefore their challenge. As the facts became clearer, most of the citizens of Poplar Bluff began to be aware of an inner desire to do something—to take some action to get to work.

A combination of factors were involved: a sense of pride, and an awareness of personal responsibility, and of the fact that whatever hurt or held back or degraded any person or family in the community, affected everybody living there.

The discussions became more organized. Committees were formed. Special meetings were held. The city fathers were questioned, argued with, and badgered with requests for information. Some considered calling in outside experts, but they couldn't afford the fees. Finally it became clear that if they wanted to do something, they would have to do it themselves—not just some of them, but all of them would have to participate.

They were unsure how to begin. Most of the people were loaded with good intentions but had no idea of how to convert those intentions into action.

Some of these people had heard of the Dale Carnegie Course and what it had done for business or personal acquaintances and they thought: "If it could change the direction of the lives of people we know, why can't those principles help change our town?"

The local Kiwanis Club agreed to cooperate in the presentation of a Dale Carnegie Course. A nucleus of business and professional people participated. As the course progressed word spread that something new and important was happening in and to Poplar Bluff. People who had not spoken up before began to make themselves heard. Their confidence and enthusiasm began to permeate the rest of the community. Good ideas were brought up—and people listened.

One who spoke up was F. O. ("Pete") Gloriod, the manager of the local theater. Pete was a member of the Kiwanis Club and served on the Kiwanis committee to develop better civic programs. It was Pete and his committee that had brought the Dale Carnegie Course to town.

Within a short time a surging force was turned loose. Here was a new beginning, a new program, a program that could enlist the support and cooperation of everybody.

This mushroomed into a phenomenon unprecedented in community affairs. Within a matter of days more than two hundred people signed up for the Course, including elected officials, merchants, doctors, business people, women's club leaders, high school students, housewives, highway patrolmen and even the chief forest ranger for the district.

After the first few sessions, when the members naturally talked about their own lives, the class talks revolved about the town and its problems. People began to learn about their neighbors and to understand their hopes and goals. Unknown or undetected qualities came out in the class members, many of whom could be enlisted into participating in the overall objective of improving and saving Poplar Bluff.

Encouraged by all that was happening in this new perspective, the people of the town began to look at themselves in fresh and exciting terms. They were no longer a backwash, no longer a lost world without purpose or plan or destiny or

dream. They were a people with a surge of faith in themselves and what they could do.

"We began to stand up and talk," one young pharmacist,
among the first to graduate from the course, declared. "It
was not easy—but the Carnegie approach was designed, we
came to understand, to do away with fear right away."

It didn't matter whether they had ever before been in
front of an audience. They had to put fear aside because
they had something important to say and to do. Suddenly
they realized that here was a course that was created and
evolved for the purpose of guiding human beings to something better, something that was actually meaningful for
themselves, their families, their future.

"First we talked about ourselves," one young man recalled,
"then we began talking about the town and what ought to be
done. Pretty soon we were talking about who ought to do it."

That, it turned out, was one of the easiest of all decisions
they had to make. Who was going to do these things that
had to be done? *Why, it was themselves.*

Among the graduates of the first class was a thirty-three-
year-old local truck salesman named John West. John and
his associates decided that the first step in the campaign to
revitalize Poplar Bluff was to elect a mayor who would be
100 percent behind their program. The incumbent had been
a do-nothing mayor and a representative of the old complacent group that had let Poplar Bluff decline. John was chosen to run against him. With the support of his Carnegie
classmates and his ability to express his ideas clearly and enthusiastically, he was easily elected.

Upon taking office, John West launched the first of the
programs designed to reshape the city. Needs had to be met,
funds had to be found. Among the projects needed to be
tackled was the rebuilding of the sewer system, the building
of a power plant which would cost $1.2 million, paving the

streets and building new roads at a cost of another $2 million. The newly elected mayor and council passed the necessary legislation to get these projects under way.

Another Dale Carnegie graduate, Lou Snyder, the proprietor of a Poplar Bluff supermarket, was named chairman of the town's sewer committee. To get this major project passed and monies allocated and raised required a vote by the people of the town.

Normally a quiet, shy young man, Snyder turned into a firebrand of purpose. He gave public talks and then went from door-to-door, from one home to the next, explaining in detail and making certain that the people of Poplar Bluff understood the full import of this first major step forward. His enthusiasm and quiet self-confidence made his acceptance by the people much easier. When the vote for a new sewer system was taken, the people of Poplar Bluff passed it by three to one.

Installing adequate sewage made the town eligible for federal aid and for a Public Housing Authority program to replace the rotting and substandard housing. Poplar Bluff's leaders—many of whom had never spoken to anyone in a higher position than a clerk—met with government leaders in Washington and came back with a $2.5 million grant for housing.

Pete Gloriod and a committee of forty-five townspeople launched a program to attract business into Poplar Bluff. They made their debut at the Industrial Development Conference held in Jefferson City, the state capital. Poplar Bluff's delegation was larger than those from the two major cities of the state, St. Louis and Kansas City. Industry began to notice Poplar Bluff.

The committee did not limit itself to talking or to mailing circulars to prospective industrial employers. Under the auspices of the Chamber of Commerce—headed by Carnegie graduates—they formed a unique organization known as: Poplar Bluff Industries. Headed by W. H. ("Bud") Toellner, this organization built houses and leased them to private industry for the use of their employees. Since one of the reasons industry was reluctant to open facilities in Poplar Bluff had been lack of housing, this new housing program encouraged several firms to build plants there, thus opening up jobs for almost six hundred people.

Just as John West saw the need to bring new life to the city administration, other Carnegie graduates ran for and were elected to the school board. Through their efforts a $1.3 million bond issue was passed enabling the construction of new senior and junior high schools.

New private building followed. Six hundred and fifty thousand dollars was raised for the construction of new hospital facilities and other improvements. Local churches took over the responsibility of raising one million dollars for new construction. Private companies enlarged or modernized their facilities. A new subdivision of ranch homes was constructed in the town.

Even Poplar Bluff's tiny airport was expanded. A new administration building and four T-hangars were built. The newly appointed airport commissioner, Pete Gloriod, who had been so active in furthering the project, made this promise: "We are now able to handle the private plane traffic so necessary to our industrial growth, and we're determined to get regular airline service in here soon."

What did the Dale Carnegie Course do for the people of Poplar Bluff?

"It gave me the courage to stand up and speak out" says Lou Snyder.

"It showed me how to fire up enthusiasm in my home town . . . and it paid off in results" says Pete Gloriod.

"It helped me learn to change minds without offending," was the comment of garden club president, Mrs. Ellery Pool.

"Our rebirth of community initiative was largely inspired by our more than two hundred Dale Carnegie graduates," said Mayor John West. "They generated interest and secured support for civic improvements and industrial expansion that benefit the entire community. We're mighty glad the Dale Carnegie Course came to Poplar Bluff."

4

Speaking in Public

Is there the faintest shadow of a reason why you should not be able to think as well in a perpendicular position before an audience as you can sitting down? Is there any reason why you should play host to butterflies in your stomach and become a victim of the "trembles" when you get up and address an audience? Surely, you realize that this condition can be remedied, that training and practice will wear away your audience-fright and give you self-confidence. —DALE CARNEGIE

Otto Kossuth, a Michigan businessman commented: "I owe my business success to the Dale Carnegie Course. I had been in manufacturing and became a plant manager, and then general manager of the division. Top management wanted someone who knew manufacturing to talk on the various products we produced and they asked me if I would participate in this program. Before I took the Dale Carnegie Course I would have found some excuse to refuse, but now I was enthusiastic and eager to make these talks. I told management I would do it and was invited to Detroit to discuss the matter with the executives there. The result was that they put me in charge of all the presentations for the company products and for arranging meetings all over the country. I made in-plant and public presentations. The reason I had no difficulty doing this, and indeed, enjoyed every minute of it, is that the little talks I had given during the Course had given me confidence. Throughout all the talks, I had the opportunity to use the tools for communication I had developed, and it proved to be a very satisfying experience."

Like Otto Kossuth, many men and women start with great

reluctance or even fear of expressing themselves before a group. Until this can be overcome, their business, social and personal growth can be seriously impaired.

Early in his career, Dale Carnegie recognized that overcoming this fear would have a profound effect on people. In his college days he had been a debater and had experienced his share of butterflies in his stomach but with practice and application he had overcome this fear to the extent that he really enjoyed speaking and reciting in public.

Back in 1912 when Dale Carnegie began his career as a teacher of public speaking, the objective was to master the kind of golden-tongued oratory which flourished in those pre-radio/television days. Most men and women who wanted to learn how to express themselves with ease and self-confidence would not spend time and money studying the mechanics of speech, of voice production, and the rules of rhetoric and formalized gestures. Dale Carnegie's courses in effective speaking were successful because they gave people the direct results they wanted.

"My first class was small," Mr. Carnegie recalled. "I taught pretty much the conventional stuff I had learned in college, but soon I began to see that that wasn't what my students— average young people trying to get ahead; clerks, secretaries, salespeople and mechanics—really wanted and needed. It wouldn't help the person trying to sell insurance to puff out his cheeks and recite a Shakespearean soliloquy, however eloquently.

"I began to see that the chief trouble was fear—fear of getting up on one's feet before a lot of people, fear of standing there alone and talking.

"I decided to get rid of that fear by making everyone talk, however briefly at every meeting. I soon found that they were teaching themselves ten times as much as I could ever teach them."

The emotional state of Dale Carnegie's early class

members was much the same as those of today—ranging from those who are ill at ease, to those who suffer downright terror. He told of a student in one of his classes who collapsed to the floor in a dead faint when he started his first talk. Quickly, Dale bounded on to the platform, and dramatically pointing to the fallen figure, announced: "One month from today, this man will make a speech from this platform." And the man did.

Once the initial fear is overcome—and it usually takes only a few weeks—participants not only don't hesitate to make their class talks, but often go out of their way to seek opportunities to talk. Dale Carnegie told of a Wall Street man who was so self-conscious at board meetings he was too shy to second a motion. When he enrolled in the Course he was seized with such terror when called upon to introduce himself that he ran out of the room. Desperately in need of help he came back. After a few sessions he began to enjoy the new experience. Early one Sunday morning he shook his wife awake and asked: "Is there any place in New York where I can make a speech today?" She reminded him that anyone could speak at a Quaker meeting if the spirit moved him. Somewhere in Brooklyn he located a Quaker meeting house and was so moved by the spirit that he spoke for twenty minutes.

What is the secret of Carnegie's success in making confident speakers of people who, only a few short weeks prior to starting the Course, could not even bear the thought of uttering a word in public, to say nothing of delivering a talk?

He summarizes it succinctly in his booklet, *Speak More Effectively* which is given to all those taking the Course: "Talk about something that you have earned the right to talk about through long study or experience. Talk about something you know and *know* that you know. Don't spend ten minutes or ten hours preparing a talk—spend ten weeks or ten months. Better still, spend ten *years*. Talk about something that has aroused your interest. Talk about something that you have a deep desire to communicate to your listeners."

"There was a chemical engineer in one of my classes," Carnegie recalled "who talked one night on 'The Menace of Communism'. It was a dreary performance. I asked him how he happened to choose the subject. 'I read an editorial about it in one of the newspapers,' he said. 'It sounded like it,' I said. 'You aren't any more afraid of Communism than you are of the bogey man. You've never been to Russia. You have no first-hand knowledge. Stick to what you know and understand.' Later in the course he made a cracking good talk on sulphuric acid. Can you image a duller subject? But he was interested in it, and what was more, he found a way to connect it with the interests of the members of his audience. He showed how almost everything a person uses from the early morning until late at night—bathtub, toothbrush, newspapers, clothes, knives and forks, automobiles, books—owes its manufacture at least in part to sulphuric acid."

Dale Carnegie wrote that it is difficult (if not impossible) to teach a person *how* to communicate. "We can best succeed in helping the person to *want* or *desire* to communicate. If the *eagerness* to 'share' or communicate is great enough, then communication itself will naturally follow. Our job in this course is to intensify this desire."

This is accomplished by inspiring every student with the eager desire to make his talk. Carnegie followed John Dewey's belief that "the deepest urge in human nature is to be important." Each class member can achieve this desire by making the talk before his classmates and the instructor. This gives the student a feeling of importance, which is well deserved, for the courage and the wish to improve himself. The instructor augments this feeling of importance by sincere and meaningful comments which further assure the speaker.

In typical "public speaking" courses in colleges, high schools and adult education programs, a good deal of emphasis is placed on developing outlines, and making notes, on proper breath control, on the use of the hands, on platform posture, and on similar matters. Carnegie avoids all of these. Participants are encouraged to be relaxed in their presentation. Gestures will come naturally from the feeling the speaker has about the subject. No notes are ever used in a talk and all talks are limited to two minutes. Some critics have felt that a two-minute talk is not really good preparation for the longer talks one may be called upon to make in business or other activities. Carnegie instructors explain that a talk longer than two minutes is really just a series of short talks organized into a pattern.

In preparing for a talk the speaker is cautioned never to write it out. Written language is apt to be rather stilted, while conversational language flows easily.

Memorizing a talk is prohibited. If one memorizes a talk it is likely to be forgotten. Even if the speaker does not forget it, it will sound mechanical. For longer talks (not in the class) brief notes may be used to assure that major points are not out of sequence or are forgotten, but reading a speech or memorizing it takes away the fresh impact. Some students, in the early sessions, try to get by with memorized speeches. John Spindler, who became a Carnegie executive and is now retired, gave a talk before a Los Angeles class when Dale Carnegie was present. He recalls: "I had not gone more than one sentence into my talk when Mr. Carnegie flagged me down to let me know that my talk was memorized. He asked me to return to my seat and to think of an experience in my life that made such an impression on me that I could be awakened out of a sound sleep to tell it to a friend without any preparation.

Today an instructor would not handle this type of problem in that manner. Walter McTernan, a Garden City, New

York, instructor, tells of the nineteen-year-old girl who froze when her memorized talk completely evaporated from her memory. He asked her to think of an incident she would like to share with the class. The girl sobbed "I can't think of anything at all, my mind is a complete blank." Walt smiled at her and asked, "Did you go to your senior prom in high school?" The student's face lit up as she nodded affirmatively. "Tell us about it," Walt coaxed gently. She then started to talk and had to be stopped by the bell when the two minutes were up.

Students are advised to use illustrations and specific examples in their talks. They help to clarify abstract ideas and through them audiences are more likely to remember what is said. Carnegie used this principle in his writing. His books are filled with anecdotes, and examples and incidents that support the points he wants to make.

In a session of the Dale Carnegie Course on Long Island, New York, a class member who was a veterinarian illustrated his talk with an egg crate full of baby animals. There were two cocker spaniel puppies—two weeks old, a couple of hamsters, a kitten and a guinea pig. While waiting to be used for illustrative purposes, the animals stayed in their cramped quarters without a whimper. The class wondered why. The veterinarian gave them the reason: Animals, like human beings, are born without fear or hatred of other animals. Only by association with their elders do they learn prejudice, suspicion, fear and hatred. Illustrations, examples, demonstrations and exhibits do more to make a point than lengthy rhetoric.

Know forty times as much about your subject as you can use is a phrase often repeated in Carnegie circles. Thorough knowledge of a subject makes the speaker more at ease, provides confidence and the ability to share information.

In the succinct booklet, *Speak More Effectively*, **Dale Carnegie** emphasizes the concern that so many speakers have about how they look and come across to an audience: "The truth is," he writes "that when you face an audience you should forget all about voice, breathing, gestures, posture, emphasis. Forget everything except what you are saying. Do what a cat does when she is trying to catch a mouse. She doesn't look around and say 'I wonder how my tail looks and I wonder if I'm standing right, and how is my facial expression?' Oh, no. The cat is so intent on catching a mouse for dinner that she couldn't stand wrong or look wrong if she tried—and neither can you if you are so vitally interested in your audience and in what you are saying that you forget yourself."

Each speaker is greeted with applause before beginning the talk, and again at the finish. Applause is an important part of Carnegie training. It is a sign of approval, appreciation and recognition. Applause gives the speaker a feeling of confidence and gives the audience a feeling of participation and enthusiasm.

Phil Deane, who presented the first Dale Carnegie courses in Venezuela, tells the story of a session he held in Caracas. When he arrived at the hotel there was a message from the manager asking to see him. "He told me that we would not be able to meet tonight. The president of Venezuela was attending a meeting down the hall and had demanded absolute silence. 'With all of your applauding and hollering, I just cannot let you meet here,' said the manager. I responded that we had people coming from great distances to this class, and with no notice of cancellation it would cause considerable inconvenience.

" 'If I promised that we wouldn't make any noise, could we hold the meeting?' I asked. He said: 'No, because the least amount of disturbance would bring someone down from the president's party and make you stop.' I asked him if we promised not to applaud, could we hold the meeting. He reluctantly agreed.

"When the class assembled I told them the problem and indicated that under no circumstances could we applaud or make any noise that evening. After five speakers had given their talks without applause, we could feel the difference in the atmosphere of the class. The speakers were not coming across enthusiastically; the audience was becoming inattentive and restless. The atmosphere of approval, which is a hallmark of Carnegie classes, just wasn't there. So finally, I said: 'Just to show our speakers we are interested, let's tap our fingers silently together after each talk.' You have never seen such enthusiastic silent activity—and the true Carnegie spirit returned to the class."

In addition to the opportunities for making speeches, the Course requires class members to take part in several impromptu talk exercises. James Sulcer, manager of manpower development for a large insurance company, tells how this helped him: "I was called to a meeting in one of our divisions and I assumed there were going to be three or four people present. When I arrived at the meeting twenty-five people were there. They were waiting for me and there was no introduction other than 'This is Jim Sulcer'. It so happened that the door by which I entered was at the other end of the room from the head table so I had some distance to walk to the dais. Those few seconds helped me a bit, but I must say that the impromptu speaking training in the Course gave me the confidence and the know-how, so I went right up there and did a good job."

Giving talks is not the only way the Dale Carnegie Course helps in improving communication. Another approach is the use of group communication such as conferences and meetings.

The major thrust of these sessions is to show class members how to get to the point rapidly and encourage others to avoid wasting time and words at meetings. They are told of the formula developed by Leon Shimkin, chairman of the board of Simon and Schuster.

"For fifteen years I spent almost half of every business day holding conferences, discussing problems. Should we do this or that—do nothing at all? We would get tense; twist in our chairs; walk the floor; argue and go around in circles. When night came, I would be utterly exhausted. . . . Finally I devised a plan that eliminated this. I have been using this plan for many years and it has performed wonders for my efficiency, my health and my happiness. . . .

"Here is the secret: First, I immediately stopped the procedure I had been using in my conferences for fifteen years—a procedure that began with my troubled associates reciting all the details of what had gone wrong, and that ended by asking 'What shall we do?'. Second, I made a new rule—a rule that everyone who wishes to present a problem to me must first prepare and submit a memorandum answering these four questions:

"Question 1: What is the problem?

("In the old days we used to spend an hour or two in a worried conference without anyone's knowing specifically and concretely what the real problem was. We used to work ourselves into a lather discussing our troubles without ever troubling to write out specifically what our problem was.)

"Question 2: What are the causes of the problem?

("As I look back over my career, I am appalled at the wasted hours I spent in worried conferences without ever trying to find out clearly the conditions which lay at the root of the problem.)

"Question 3: What are the possible solutions?

("In the old days, one man in the conference would suggest one solution. Someone else would argue with him. Tempers would flare. We would often get clear off the subject and at the end of the conference, no one would have written down all the various things we could do to attack the problem.)

"Question 4: What is the best possible solution?

("I used to go into a conference with a man who had spent long hours worrying about a situation without ever once thinking through all the possible solutions and then writing down: 'This is the solution I recommend.')

"My associates rarely come to me now with their problems. Why? Because they have discovered that in order to answer those four questions, they have to get all the facts and think their problem through. And after they have done that they find, in three-fourths of the cases, they don't have to consult me at all, because the proper solution has popped out like a piece of bread popping out of an electric toaster. Even in those cases where consultation is necessary, the discussion takes about one-third the time formerly required because it proceeds along an orderly, logical path to a reasoned conclusion."[1]

These principles are applied in conferences held in the classroom. Reading about how to handle a problem is only the first step. The students now apply the four steps to a problem, chosen in one session and worked out at the next one. They are guided in how to present their ideas clearly and forcefully and how to listen to and evaluate the other participants.

Many companies have made this formula part of their policies and procedures. It not only works in conferences but also in any type of communication concerning problems within an organization.

Dale Carnegie liked to take on tough challenges and he enjoyed working with engineers. "How do you transform an engineer, absorbed in inanimate things into a manager of people?" he asked at a meeting of engineers in New York. "I

[1] Dale Carnegie, *How to Stop Worrying and Start Living* (New York: Simon and Schuster, 1944), pp. 37–39.

would rather teach engineers than any other group," he said. Many companies that employ technical people agree with Carnegie. If the ideas and creativity bottled up in these technical brains could be released by improving their ability to communicate, what a boon it would be!

F. A. Hildenbrand, president of Atlantic Richfield of Canada, Ltd., heads one of the many companies that use the Dale Carnegie programs to make their people more articulate. "Our people are technically oriented," he states. "They are geologists, engineers and legal specialists. Each of our projects requires the expenditure of considerable sums of money. We have to have very thorough reviews in committee, which requires the person who has done the work to make a detailed and clearly stated presentation. It is my contention that the ability to communicate is one of the big weaknesses in practically all of our educational programs, particularly in training technically oriented people. The Dale Carnegie Course has helped our people to make clearer presentations, with stronger conviction. They organize their material better, are at ease with their audience, and field questions are handled more effectively."

Alumni of the Carnegie Course often go out of their way to seek opportunities to use their newly acquired speaking skills. They become active members of religious and civic groups; they take on added assignments on their jobs or join a club like the Toastmasters, that meets regularly to give each member an opportunity to deliver a talk. They enjoy the experience of being in front of an audience; it enriches their lives by giving them that highly desirable feeling of importance.

People from all walks of life have found the abilities acquired during the Course helpful in their personal lives. Testimonials from thousands of people are filed in the offices of Carnegie sponsors throughout the world as well as their international headquarters. Senators, governors and other office holders credit the Course with helping them to become better speakers and in enabling them to progress in their careers. Business executives attribute their success to their ability to speak in public. Men and women who took the Course write how they are able to communicate with ease both in public and in their private lives.

Many students have reported that they even feared to really communicate with their families. Joe Carpenter of Baton Rouge, Louisiana, found that when he wanted to have a good talk with his wife he was unable to get very far. "After one of the sessions I returned home and told my wife: 'We've been wanting to have a talk, so let's have one.' And we did. We sat down and talked until we went plumb to sleep. There wasn't anything to it. From that time on we have communicated much better, and by this means our life and our marriage have improved."

Why does the Carnegie way work? One student, Dennis Lane of Chicago, pondered this question. "You go in there and throw yourself into the Course. You observe the people in the class and sit in the audience while they are speaking. As they speak you become conscious of their strengths and weaknesses, and as you speak, they become conscious of yours. You are evaluated by your peers at each meeting. This is stimulating and rewarding and it carries over into other activities of your life after you have completed the Course."

Countless class members around the world tell how the confidence developed in the courses and particularly the ability to express themselves in public have helped them in their careers. Ben Pieters, a graduate of the Dale Carnegie Course in Durban, South Africa, told about his change of attitude toward speaking in public:

"Believe it or not, I have sung in Rome in the opera house. I gave encore after encore with people standing and cheering me. I have been in Hollywood, where I have told jokes and made people roar with laughter. I have given speeches in the City Hall that have influenced the politics of our town. Unfortunately, all of this took place in my imagination!

"The turning point came last year. My boss asked me to give a lecture to the staff. I had never spoken before an audience before. I had a fluttery stomach, popped tranquilizers into my mouth and shook with fear all day. When I got up to speak my lips were dry, and I could hardly say anything. I *read* my lecture from notes—it was bad.

"This year, two weeks ago, I was again asked to give a lecture to this group. I gave it and enjoyed it. I spoke for an hour to an attentive and receptive audience. While my material was as good in the previous lecture, I had presented it badly, and I myself was a nervous wreck. This time, after my Dale Carnegie training, I was at ease and my boss and others complimented me on the way I delivered my talk."

The ability to express oneself is stressed in all Dale Carnegie courses. Public speaking may be only a small part of communication, yet it is through public speaking that self-confidence, enthusiasm and ability to communicate with others on a person-to-person basis is developed. Those who have taken the Dale Carnegie courses have little to fear in making a talk. In fact, many graduates go out of their way in seeking opportunities to talk in public. While some may have little opportunity to speak before an audience after they have completed their course, all will be able to make an acceptable speech with confidence when the need or opportunity arises. As one graduate commented: "The butterflies may still be there, but now they fly in formation."

5

Generating Enthusiasm

Enthusiasm is the dynamics of your personality. Without it, whatever abilities you may possess lie dormant; and it is safe to say that nearly every man has more latent power than he ever learns to use. You may have knowledge, sound judgment, good reasoning faculties; but no one—not even yourself—will know it until you discover how to put your heart into thought and action. —DALE CARNEGIE

Stan Novak of Cleveland, Ohio, came home from work to find his youngest son, Tim, kicking and screaming on the living room floor. He was to start kindergarten the next day and was protesting that he would not go. Stan's normal reaction was to banish the child to his room and tell him he'd just better make up his mind to go. Recognizing that this would not really help Tim start kindergarten in the best frame of mind, Stan determined to apply what he had learned in his Dale Carnegie Course. He sat down and thought, "If I were Tim why would I be excited about going to kindergarten?" He and his wife made a list of all the fun things Tim would do such as finger painting, singing songs, making new friends, and so forth. Then they put them into action. "We all started finger painting on the kitchen table; Lil, my wife, my other son Bob, and myself, all having fun. Soon Tim was peeping around the corner. Next he was begging to participate. 'Oh, no! you have to go to kindergarten first to learn how to finger paint.' With all the enthusiasm I could muster I went through the list talking in terms he could understand—telling him all the fun he would have in kindergarten. The next morning, I was the first one up. I went downstairs and found Tim sitting sound asleep in the living room chair. 'What are you doing here?', I asked. 'I'm waiting to go to kindergarten. I don't want to be late.' The enthusiasm of our entire family had aroused in Tim the eager want to go to kindergarten that no amount of discussion or threat could have possibly accomplished."

If there is one ingredient of success that surpasses all others, it is *enthusiasm,* according to Dale Carnegie. He always spoke of this, travelling around the country, over the radio, and in private meetings with his instructors. In these talks, he often reflected on his own life, and how the magic of enthusiasm contributed to his success. People who heard Carnegie speak often commented that he was not a polished orator, nor did he have the diction one expected from a "speech expert." The enthusiasm that emanated from him, however, captured the audience from the start, and he never lost their interest until he finished.

Carnegie carried this enthusiasm into his teaching. He became so excited about seeing those who took his courses making progress, that it often happened he couldn't go home right after a session, but would keep on reviewing it with his colleagues at a local cafeteria long into the evening.

Enthusiasm is an inner excitement that permeates the whole being. The word comes from two Greek roots: *en* meaning *in* and *theos* meaning *God.* Literally, the person with enthusiasm has God within. It is an inner glow—an ardent, spiritual quality deep down inside a person.

Development of enthusiasm in individuals, groups, athletic teams, companies and total communities pays off in positive action, in success and happiness. This can be observed in athletic competitions. One of the great football coaches of all time was Vince Lombardi. Norman Vincent Peale tells this story in his booklet: *Enthusiasm: What It Can Do for You.*[1]

---

[1] Norman Vincent Peale, *Enthusiasm* (Pawling, New York: Foundation for Christian Living, 1973), pp. 26–27.

"When he (Lombardi) came to Green Bay he faced a defeated, dispirited team. He stood before them, looked them over silently for a long time and then in a quiet but intense voice said, 'Gentlemen, we are going to have a great football team. We are going to win games. Get that. You are going to learn to block. You are going to learn to run. You are going to learn to tackle. You are going to outplay the teams that come against you. Get that.

" 'And how is this to be done?" he continued. 'You are to have confidence in me and enthusiasm for my system. The secret of the whole matter will be what goes on up here (and he tapped his temple). Hereafter, I want you to think of only three things: your home, your religion and the Green Bay Packers, in that order! Let enthusiasm take hold of you!'

"The men sat up straight in their chairs. 'I walked out of that meeting,' writes the quarterback, 'feeling ten feet tall.' That year they won seven games—with virtually the same players who had lost ten games the year before. The next year they won a division title and the third year the world championship. Why? Because, added to hard work and skill and love of the sport, enthusiasm made the difference."

Peale goes on to say: "What happened to the Green Bay Packers can happen to a church, to a business, to a country, to an individual. What goes on in the mind is what determines outcome. When an individual really gets enthusiasm, you can see it in the flash of his eyes, in his alert and vibrant personality. You observe it in the spring of his step. You can see it in the verve of his whole being. Enthusiasm makes the difference in his attitude toward other people, toward his job, toward the world. It makes a great big difference in the zest and delight of human existence."

Dale Carnegie often quoted Frederick Williamson, onetime president of the New York Central Railroad: "The longer I live, the more certain I am that *enthusiasm is the little-recognized secret of success*. The difference in actual skill and ability and intelligence between those who succeed and those who fail is usually not very great. But if two men are about equally matched, the man who is enthusiastic will have more in his favor. And a man of modest ability, who possesses enthusiasm will often outstrip one who has first-rate ability, but no enthusiasm." Carnegie felt that this statement reflected his own ideas so clearly that he wrote a booklet on the importance of enthusiasm. This succinct essay on enthusiasm is given to all the class members who participate in the Dale Carnegie Course.

Enthusiasm is not skin-deep. It must emanate from within a person. It rarely can be feigned for a sustained period of time. One way of generating a continuing surge of enthusiasm is to set a goal, work toward it and, when it is accomplished, set another goal and work toward it. The excitement and challenge this provides cannot help but keep one enthusiastic.

James Nentwig took the Dale Carnegie Sales Course in Minneapolis in the early 1960s. At the time, he was selling life insurance for the John Hancock Insurance Company. He was so enthusiastic about the course that when he was transferred by his company to St. Louis, Missouri, he approached Redd Storey, the Carnegie manager there and volunteered to be a group leader (a graduate who assists the instructor). Eventually, he qualified as an instructor himself.

One evening after class Jim gave Redd Storey a lift in his Volkswagen. Storey noticed that he had pasted a picture of a Cadillac on his dashboard. Nentwig said: "Every time I get into this car I look at this picture and I say to myself, 'Jim, someday you're going to drive that car.' "

In a year Jim was promoted to staff manager. He built up a tremendously productive staff in St. Louis and was able to buy that Cadillac. However, he was still not satisfied. He went to his boss and said he wouldn't be happy for long in the work he was doing. "I want your job or one like it, before the end of the year or I'll quit." He was so valuable as staff manager that they didn't want to lose him. At the beginning of the following year he was made branch manager in Tulsa, Oklahoma, where previously they had had no office, no sales force and no customers. In one year he had forty-two salespeople, and was setting all kinds of records for the company.

Then they transferred him to the Boston headquarters and made him field training manager responsible for setting up offices all over the country. In another year they transferred him back to St. Louis as regional vice president. At that time he had just turned thirty. Wherever he was, when his travel schedule allowed, he taught the Dale Carnegie Sales Course. Still in his early thirties, Jim Nentwig has been transferred again—this time as a corporate vice president of his company.

Men and women like Jim Nentwig, who are enthusiastic and excited about everything they do, are the kind of people chosen to teach the Sales Course. Successful in selling or managing salespeople they take the time and effort to undergo the necessary rigorous training for Carnegie Instructors.

In one of the Junior Achievement classes in New Brighton, Pennsylvania, Chris Kati reported how setting a goal helped bring her project to a successful conclusion. The project was selling first aid kits and at the end of the year they had three hundred sets left over. They could sell them back to the drug store from which they purchased them, but this would leave them with a deficit and the stockholders would get no dividends. They held a meeting and Chris read them an inspirational poem which had been read earlier in the Course. The J.A. group agreed to get out and make a strong effort to sell the balance of the kits. Their new enthusiasm enabled them to sell one hundred sets in the remaining week of the school term and thus meet all their obligations, with enough profit for a small dividend for the stockholders.

Enthusiasm will drive people out of their lethargy to do things. Dr. W. A. Cabaluna of Chateaugay, New York, tells of his frustration when he tried to get support for the county chapter of the American Cancer Society: "Every idea, every proposal I made met with comments like 'we tried that before and it didn't work' or 'nobody's interested.' I flared up, embittered, angered. The next morning I picked up the phone and called people. About a week ago, I spoke to the medical staff of my hospital. Instead of just sitting at the table as I usually did, I stood up and presented my arguments with enthusiasm. I wasn't shouting or jumping around, but showed sincerity, zeal, earnestness, and willingness to pursue a goal. The feeling cannot be adequately described, but it could be seen in the close attention and facial reactions of my audience. The results were the beginning of an active campaign to help in this important program in our community."

Skeptical class members want to know how they can become enthusiastic about something like an unpleasant chore they must do or a subject about which they know little and care less.

Just as they had been advised to conquer fear by doing what they feared most, it was suggested that they tackle the things they are less interested in first, and by working hard, they will discover it is not as dull or as difficult as they thought.

"How can a student become five times more enthusiastic?" Dale Carnegie was often asked this question by his instructors. In a memo to his colleague, Murray Mosser, Carnegie explained this:

"First, force yourself to *act* enthusiastic and you will tend to *be* enthusiastic.

"Second, delve into your subject, study it, learn it, live it.

Get as much information as you can about it. That will often unconsciously make you more enthusiastic. For example, I was not very enthusiastic about Lincoln until I wrote a book about him. Now I am intensely enthusiastic about him. George Washington may have been just as great a man but I am not as enthusiastic about him because I do not know as much about him. You can get enthusiastic only about a subject you know well.

"I have two neighbors, one of whom is an appraiser. If you can get him to talk on that subject he will talk all day. The other neighbor is a famous sculptor. He can get enthusiastic about sculpturing at the snap of a finger, yet he could not get enthusiastic about appraising.

"Another example: my wife, Dorothy, is not enthusiastic about Abraham Lincoln because she knows little about him, but she is almost an authority on Shakespeare, so she gets animated and excited about him. I cannot be one-third as excited about Shakespeare about whom I know little, as I can about Lincoln, about whom I know much.

"What is enthusiasm? It is really an outward manifestation of an inward feeling. Let's place our emphasis on having people talk about their deep and moving interests. If we can do that, the speaker will use animation as unconsciously as he breathes. Let's do all of our teaching from the inside."

Carnegie cautions that enthusiasm should not be confused with noise, volume, shouting, yelling. He continues "When I speak of enthusiasm I refer to an ardent spiritual quality, deep down inside. . . . I like to call it 'suppressed excitement'. If your heart is on fire with a desire to help others, you will be excited. Your excitement will radiate through your eyes, your face, your soul and your whole personality. You will be inspired; and your inspiration will inspire others."

Good physical conditioning is a sound basis for generating enthusiasm. If one is energetic in an activity, mental and emotional energy result. Many salespeople, teachers, business executives, professional people and others start their day with such physical exercise as calisthenics, jogging and bicycling. Not only does this improve health, but it provides a boost to the level of energy and enthusiasm for the day's activities.

Another means of developing enthusiasm is a pep talk or a few encouraging words before undertaking an activity. Pep talks, of course, have been used by sport coaches to motivate their teams; by sales managers to motivate their staffs; and by many others concerned with group activities. While a pep talk to oneself is not usual, it can be very effective, and do for the individual what the coach's talk does for the team. The Dale Carnegie program encourages class members to give themselves pep talks. Salespeople who give themselves pep talks before seeing a prospect make better sales presentations and close more sales. One class member reported he gave himself a pep talk before he proposed to his fiancee.

A New York graduate told how being enthusiastic won her a new job. She had completed secretarial school and was seeking a position as a medical secretary. After a few rejections because of her lack of work experience in this field, she began to apply the principles of enthusiasm she had learned in the Course. On the way to another interview she gave herself a pep talk. "I want this job," she said. "I have the technical know-how. I am a diligent and conscientious worker. I can do the job and will be a real asset to this doctor." She repeated this over and over on the way to the doctor's office. She confidently entered the office and answered the doctor's questions with such enthusiasm that he offered her the job. Some months later he told her that when he saw from her application form that she did not have any experience he had decided just to give her a courtesy interview and reject her, but her enthusiasm convinced him to try her. She carried that enthusiasm into the work itself and was a very successful medical secretary.

Lewis Conrad of Grand Rapids, Michigan, tells of failing to sell a furnace to a prospect. After taking the Course he went back to that prospect and made the sale. The purchaser said, "I'm sure glad I didn't buy the furnace you tried to sell me last time you were here. This sounds like a much better furnace." Lewis commented: "It was the same furnace—just a more enthusiastic sales presentation."

A South African class member, Aif McEwan, applied the concept of enthusiasm to opening one of the toughest accounts in his industry. He represented a company that leases cranes to contractors. The customer, whom he called "Mr. Smith," was always rude and usually in a violent temper. After two calls in which Smith refused to listen to his presentation, McEwan made another attempt to see him. McEwan described the scene: "He was again in a violent mood, standing in front of his desk shouting at another salesman. Mr. Smith's face was as red as a tomato; the other poor salesman was trembling. Instead of letting this frighten me, I determined to show my enthusiasm. It was my turn next. He shouted 'Next.' I walked into his office. He said loudly, 'You again—what do you want?' Before he could say anything else I smiled and without the tremor most salesmen had in their voices when addressing him, I said in my most enthusiastic manner, 'I would like to have all of your crane hire business.' He stood there behind his desk for fifteen seconds, speechless. He looked at me in an odd way and said, 'You sit over there and wait for me.' When he returned one-half hour later he greeted me with 'Are you still here?' I told him that I had such a good deal for him that I wouldn't think of leaving until I could explain it to him. The result was an order amounting to 75,000 rands per month for a year's contract with good possibilities of much more business."

Carnegie students radiate enthusiasm about the Course and frequently recommend it to their friends, require it of their employees or enroll their spouses, children and other relatives. In some communities Carnegie alumni meet periodically to exchange ideas on how to continue to grow through lifelong learning and to report on how this training has helped them in their lives.

Senator Paul Fannin of Arizona took the Dale Carnegie Course in the late 1940s. He was so enthusiastic with what the course did for him that he recommended the Course in many of his public speeches. He later became governor of Arizona and then senator from that state. He had his entire family take the course. His son Tom, now a very successful business executive, became an instructor and taught both the Dale Carnegie Course and the Sales Course for many years.

Many students made significant changes in their lives and their careers, through the enthusiasm they learned to release in the Dale Carnegie courses. Sue Mascia of Los Altos, California, tells of a woman in her class who had a very serious problem. She was completely backward socially and in the early classes her talks were dull. She had been married for nineteen years, but was recently divorced. Little by little she evinced more and more enthusiasm during the weeks she was taking the Course. Then she remarried. Her enthusiasm about everything she did, from decorating her home to introducing new games to her guests, made every contact with her exciting.

Another alumnus whose life was changed by the Course was Melvin S. ("Bud") Falck. When Bud took the Course he was a captain in the army. Murray Mosser, who was his instructor met with him after the session on enthusiasm. Mosser writes: "I asked him 'Bud, what do you plan to do with your life?' He answered: 'What do you mean what do I plan to do? I am a captain in the army and I expect to make a career there.' I said: 'Anybody with your outstanding leadership characteristics and the enthusiasm you exude could be a top leader in almost any field. If you set your goals and make your plans you'll succeed in almost anything.' Bud went home that night, and talked to his wife the whole night long. They drew up a long-term plan. He decided to join a mutual fund company as a part-time salesman while still in the army. When he retired he started selling mutual funds full-time. Now he has twenty-four people working for him. In addition, he is president of a life insurance company, has other financial interests and his net worth is over a million dollars. Every time I see Bud Falck I ask him what is the real secret of his success. 'Murray,' he says, 'it's enthusiasm.' "

Doug Dares, a fire fighter in Dartmouth, Nova Scotia, and a graduate of the Dale Carnegie Course, demonstrated enthusiasm when he gave a talk on fire safety to an elementary school class. He reported: "I walked into the classroom in my fire-fighting equipment: helmet, coat, hooks, spanner and socks. I gave a short talk on why we wear the equipment, plus a short diagram lesson on why not to play with matches. We then went to the library to view two movies on fire safety. After the movie, I talked in a most enthusiastic tone of a special surprise I had in mind for the children. 'I'm going to make you all honorary fire fighters! How? Well, I am going to show you how you can get your Mom, Dad, brothers, sisters, aunts, uncles, whoever, to safety when a fire occurs in your house. Now, remember! The smoke hangs from the ceiling to here (indicating about three feet from the floor) so everyone is going to crawl on hands and knees down the hall back to the classroom.' The responding cheer was stupendous. The teacher was amazed, and I was delighted. Before I could get in another word, the children were crawling down the hallway (150 feet) on their stomachs, their hands and their knees, with me watching and the teacher grinning."

Dale Carnegie felt that a prime responsibility of his in-

structors was to develop enthusiasm among the class participants by helping them generate it within themselves. One
guideline to this is to watch the miracles that are performed
in the classes. There is no better stimulus to personal enthusiasm than observing another person's success. One cannot
help being enthusiastic when one sees a classmate change
from a shy, quiet individual to one bursting with animation
and excitement.

If the instructor is not enthusiastic it is not likely that
students will become enthusiastic. Instructors are advised to
shake themselves awake and act enthusiastic throughout the
session. Students frequently comment about the excitement
generated in the classes by these energetic and enthusiastic
men and women who teach the courses.

A plaque with the following motto hung over Dale Carnegie's desk and a duplicate over his mirror at home. Coinci-
dentally, General Douglas MacArthur had the same motto
on his wall when he commanded the Allied Forces in the
South Pacific:

>You are as young as your faith,
>as old as your doubts;
>as young as your self-confidence,
>as old as your fears;
>as young as your hope,
>as old as your despair.
>Years may wrinkle the skin,
>but to give up enthusiasm
>wrinkles the soul.*

This is one of the finest tributes ever made to enthusiasm.
Through the development of this trait, people add sparkle
and zest to everything they do.

*Adapted from "Youth" by the American Writer, Samuel Ullman (1840–
1924).

6

Winning Friends
and Influencing People

You can make more friends in two months by becoming really interested in other people, than you can in two years by trying to get other people interested in you. Which is just another way of saying that the way to make a friend is to be one.

—DALE CARNEGIE

To a great many people the name Dale Carnegie is synonymous with *How to Win Friends and Influence People,* the all-time best selling book which has changed the lives of millions of readers. However, the human relations aspects of the Carnegie training was a natural growth of Mr. Carnegie's original course in effective speaking, not the other way around.

In the preface to *How to Win Friends and Influence People* Dale Carnegie wrote: "I have, since 1912, been conducting educational courses for business and professional men and women in New York. At first, I conducted courses in public speaking only—courses designed to train adults, by actual experience, to think on their feet and express their ideas with more clarity, more effectiveness, and more poise, both in business interviews and before groups.

"But gradually as the seasons passed, I realized that sorely as these adults needed training in effective speaking, they needed still more training in the fine art of getting along with people in everyday business and social contacts."

Early in his experience, Dale Carnegie discovered that to teach the principles of human relations in a manner that

109

would result in changing the way of life of people, could not be done by preaching. He had to make these principles alive in the classroom, just as he had made effective speaking an integral part of the student's total personality.

Sometimes, there is resistance to accepting the principles as laid down. A class member in Halifax County, Nova Scotia, tells of her attitude: "I came into the course pigheaded and I tried to prove that the principles taught were wrong. I bluffed my way through the first few nights, saying exactly that. I was still fighting all the way until the fourth session. I kind of let down my guard without realizing it and it just happened. I said "O.K., I'll go up and try your silly concepts." I did and it worked. So I continued trying them and it just snowballed into one big, happy feeling."

The principles are not mechanical clichés. They cannot be imposed on the student. Anyone who practices Dale Carnegie's precepts just to be liked, or to make a sale, or to influence someone, has missed the point and does an injustice to the philosophy and purpose of the Course. It just won't work that way. The participant in the course or the reader of Carnegie's books must sincerely believe in the principles set forth.

This is accomplished through the deep sincerity of the instructors, the wholehearted sharing of experiences with the class members, and the interrelationships among them. These interrelationships often become as deep and close as occurs among the members of a family.

Dan Ramsey, who took the Course in Denver, Colorado, summed it up when he said: "You can't sit in a room with forty different people and listen to them talk without realizing they are communicating and have something to say. You begin to identify with them."

This was best expressed by Roy C. Thornton of Newark, Delaware. "Another benefit I have gotten from this Course," he told his class at their final meeting, "is a belief in people;

a belief that all people are important. Listening to you—people from all walks of life, of different sexes, different races, different ages; people with different types of jobs, ranging from the student to the professional, the worker, the housewife; people with different beliefs, thoughts, ambitions, goals. I have spoken to you and you have listened; you have spoken to me and I have listened. From this I have learned to understand different beliefs and different outlooks on life. From this I have learned to respect each of you—you are deserving of this respect."

Instructors follow the principle that one of the best ways to teach is by means of association. Consciously or unconsciously, class members adopt attitudes and acquire skills by the simple process of exposure to desirable results. Instructors are trained to be sympathetic and empathetic listeners, and to serve as examples of the Carnegie principles. They are enjoined to think in terms of human relations and to speak in such terms. Thus the entire atmosphere of the class is manifested by the spirit of human relations.

Class members are asked to apply these principles in their lives. Since the results of applying these principles are always discussed in the classroom, all class members derive benefit from these discussions.

Chuck Klawitter of Bay City, Michigan, did not have one principle in mind when he determined to improve his relationship with a fellow employee with whom he had been having difficulties for years. "I used to schedule meetings with this man in the afternoon because he got me so upset that I could not get anything done the rest of the day after meeting with him. I would go home after these meetings, sick to the stomach, shaking all over. I figured it was better to shake at home in quiet than at work. I had hated this man for ten years. I was skeptical that any approach I took would change this. After looking at that card with the human relations principles printed on it twenty or thirty times, my mind changed from negative to neutral to positive. I decided to assess my relationship with this man objectively. I applied all of the rules. I stopped criticizing him, I told him how much I appreciated his suggestions and I made him feel important. The tension between us lessened and I found myself no longer getting upset during my meetings with him. In fact, I got to the point where I even enjoyed the meetings and, of course, this changed his attitude toward me. Our business relationship not only became smoother, but it added considerably to the productivity of our joint projects in our company."

Many teachers have found that by using a positive approach to the changing behavior patterns of students they get much better results than by criticizing and condemning them. Here is Dale Carnegie's first principle of human relations: *Don't criticize, condemn or complain.* It was used by Mrs. Nancy Glick, a teacher in Findlay, Ohio. She reported that at the beginning of a school year, she was upset to discover that a child who had a reputation for being a disturbing and disrupting influence in the school was to be in her class. "My first reaction was 'Oh, No!' However, I knew if I attacked this problem with a negative attitude, it would very likely end up negative. Instead, I decided that Kevin would be one of my primary goals for that school year. Instead of criticizing him, I disciplined him with a smile. For example, if he was talking to a neighbor, I'd say: 'Kevin, is there something I can do to help you?' If his work was incorrect, I would say: 'Would you like to look this over once more so I won't find any mistakes?' Sometimes when he was looking for a little mischief, I would look at him with a smile that said: 'Uh, huh, I know what you're doing.' After that he would smile and shrug his shoulders and go back to work. The change in this boy has been really miraculous. He seems very happy, he's cooperative, his work has improved and he has made two or three close friends."

Ann Sawatzky of St. Catherines, Ontario, reports: "I was an awful criticizer. I used to criticize my husband and the children for such things as leaving socks lying around or slurping the coffee. I listened to the talks in my class and realized that these little things weren't important. They solved nothing and usually created an argument that lasted for days."

Dale Carnegie said, "Criticism is futile because it puts a man on the defensive and usually makes him strive to justify himself. Criticism is dangerous, because it wounds a man's precious pride, hurts his sense of importance and arouses his resentment."

Benjamin Franklin claimed that the secret of his success as a diplomat was: "I will speak ill of no man . . . and speak all the good I know of everybody."

Instead of condemning people, Dale Carnegie recommended: "Let's try to understand them. Let's try to figure out why they do what they do. That's a lot more profitable and intriguing than criticism, and it breeds sympathy, tolerance and kindness."

Criticism can be nonverbal as well as verbal. Frederick L. Shourd of Omaha, Nebraska, told his class that when he had to select one of the human relations principles to apply as part of the preparation for one of the sessions in the Course, he went over them with his wife. "I began to read the list," he commented, "Number One: *Don't criticize, condemn or complain.* 'Well, I certainly can't use that one to improve on because I never do that.' The chandelier began to sway when my wife said, 'What!! You always complain and criticize!' 'What do you mean?' I said, 'I never do that.' 'Sure you do,' she responded. 'Don't you remember two weeks ago when you caused me to burst into tears with the sarcastic remark you made?' 'But I was only kidding', I pleaded. And then she made one of the most important comments I think anyone has ever made to me. 'But there was nothing about you that showed you were kidding. There was not a smile on your face. Nothing to indicate that you weren't completely serious.' It was at that moment that I decided that for the rest of my life I would be extremely careful with every attempted humorous remark to make sure I was communicating correctly with my body language as well as with my words."

This philosophy is the essence of the entire Dale Carnegie Course. Instructors never criticize the student. Instead, they emphasize the positive aspects of what students do and say. By deemphasizing the weaknesses, they help to build up the strengths.

Another Carnegie principle is: *Give honest, sincere appreciation.* Class members always applaud the talks given by their classmates to express their appreciation. The instructor expresses his or her appreciation by thanking the speaker and by praising the talk.

Dale Carnegie quotes Charles Schwab, the man to whom Andrew Carnegie paid a salary of $1,000,000 a year as president of U.S. Steel: "I consider my ability to arouse enthusiasm among the men the greatest asset I possess, and the way to develop the best that is in a person is by appreciation and encouragement."

William James, the great American psychologist, stated that the deepest urge in human nature is the craving to be appreciated.

Carnegie students and graduates use this principle in their daily lives. Murray Mosser, who has served the Dale Carnegie organization in various capacities for thirty years, tells of one of his earliest recollections of the application of this principle. One of his class members owned a gas station in an area where the competition was extremely keen. He was unable to make enough money to maintain his business and he could not afford to cut prices any further, nor could he spend money on advertising. He pondered this situation while preparing for his next class at Carnegie and decided to apply the principle of expressing appreciation. The next day he went over his files of credit card customers, and wrote each of them a letter thanking them for their patronage. He copied license plate numbers from transient customers, obtained their addresses, and wrote to them thanking them for stopping by.

The result was amazing. People drove into the station to thank him for the letter. Many said no businessman had ever thanked them before. A number of customers drove out of their usual route to fill up at his station. A salesman from another town would wait to get his gas until he reached the station of the man who had written the letter. All this happened despite the lower prices of the competitors in the area.

It is not just appreciation that is taught, but *sincere* appreciation. One has to really feel and believe what he or she is saying for it to come through to the other party as sincere. Dale Carnegie training has sometimes been criticized as suggesting that people fake their enthusiasm or appreciation in their personal or business relations. Dale Carnegie warned about this over and over again. If one really appreciates what someone has done, say so; if there is no appreciation, no make-believe effort will succeed, nor should it.

In Santa Ana, California, Douglas Doran, the owner of a supermarket chain, was having problems with his twenty-five-year-old son, Tom. Doran reported: "Tom was managing one of my stores and whenever I walked into that store I would find fault with everything he was doing. I expected him to run a perfect operation because he was my son. When I really evaluated his operation, I noted he had raised the volume of the store to ten thousand dollars a week, moved it from the red into the black and was well liked by his customers and employees. I had been so busy criticizing him, I hadn't ever given him credit for what he had accomplished. The next time I visited his store we walked into the back room and I told him what a great job he was doing. I specifically commented on the increase in business and complimented him on the way the customers were treated. 'If you could get everyone else here to do the same you wouldn't be able to hold all the customers you would have in here' I added. He stood there, all six-foot-five of him and the tears came into his eyes. He said 'Dad, you have never talked to me this way before in all of my life. I'm glad to know how you really feel about me.' That was the first time since he was a little shaver that I ever had really communicated with my son."

G. A. Huebner, a participant in a Dale Carnegie class in Moorhead, Minnesota, used the principle of showing sincere appreciation in a family situation. His father had been ill for many years and the burden of caring for him was shared between his mother and his brother and sister-in-law who lived in the same town. When Huebner visited his father, he took his mother aside and told her what a fine job she was doing in taking care of his father and how proud he was at the progress that had been made. He then visited his brother and sister-in-law, took them out to dinner and expressed his appreciation to them. He reported that the work and worry caused by the strain of taking care of his father had caused his family to be somewhat depressed. Showing his appreciation renewed their spirits and made them continue their efforts in caring for the sick man.

Many business executives feel that an increase in salary or a bonus is sufficient indication of appreciation for a job well done. Timothy Calvert, a businessman in Glen Arm, Maryland, wanted to do more. One of his employees had consistently produced more than others. He had given above and beyond the call of duty to his job. His bonus was more than the others received, but money did not express Calvert's feelings so he wrote him a personal letter of appreciation which he enclosed with the bonus check. In the letter he thanked him and told him how much he meant to the company. Later the employee thanked him for writing it. He said it made him cry and Calvert commented that it almost made him cry to hear him say that.

In an article published in *These Times* and condensed in the *Readers Digest,* Jane Lindstrom wrote:[1]

"Cold spring rain slashed across the window, further lowering my spirits, already depressed by long convalescence from surgery. Get-well cards had stopped coming. A faded chrysanthemum plant, a gift from my fellow teachers, was all that remained of the flowers I had received. I felt lonely, unimportant, forgotten by a world that apparently was doing very well without me.

"Then the mail arrived, bringing a note from an acquaintance, a teacher I passed every morning on my way to school. 'Dear Jane,' she wrote, 'My class is about to begin, but I must write these few words before my students arrive. I missed your smile and your wave this morning, just as I have every day since you've been ill. I pray you'll be well soon. You're probably surprised at receiving this note, but the world for me is a less happy place without you. And how will you know unless I tell you?'

"Suddenly, the paralyzing sense of despair slipped away. Someone missed me; someone needed me. That knowledge proved more effective than any medicine the doctor could prescribe."

Telling somebody that they are missed, that they are appreciated, even when there is no special event that triggers it can be a rewarding experience for both the person showing the appreciation and the person receiving it.

[1] Jane Lindstrom, "How Will You Know Unless I Tell You?" *These Times* (October 1976), as condensed in *Readers Digest* (March 1978).

"You can make more friends in two months by becoming interested in other people than you can in two years by trying to get other people interested in you."

Dale Carnegie said this in *How to Win Friends and Influence People* and he lived this in his own life. Everybody who met Carnegie remarked on his ability to become sincerely interested in whoever was with him. Murray Mosser tells of accompanying Dale Carnegie to a graduation banquet of several classes in New York City. No sooner had Dale entered the room when a class member approached him and asked him a question. He took time to listen, absorb and comment. At that moment this woman was the most important person in the room. When he left her, he was stopped by several other students. To each he gave his full attention and interest. It took forty-five minutes for Dale to reach the dais, but every person with whom he spoke felt and remembered his deep interest in them.

In an article Carnegie wrote for the *Pictorial Review* in April 1937, entitled *How to Make Your Husband's Friends Like You,* he expressed this idea succinctly:

"Ask yourself this question: 'Why should my husband's friends be interested in me unless I am first interested in them?' Write the answer to that question in the margin of this page. True, this page hasn't a wide margin; but narrow as it is, it may be wide enough to write all the honest reasons you will be able to conjure up."

He concluded the article with this advice: "The next time you meet one of your husband's friends, remember that he is ten thousand times more interested in himself and his wants and problems than he is in you and your problems. His toothache means more to him than a famine in China that kills a million people. A boil on his neck interests him more than forty earthquakes in Africa."

An old adage sums this all up. "A gossip talks about others, a bore talks about himself—and a brilliant conversationalist talks about you!"

Ann Lundin of Randolph, Massachusetts, tells of a visit she made to the Swedish Home for the Aged in West Newton. While her husband was conducting some business with the administrator, she went into the living room to wait for him. In her talk to her class she reported: "I had brought a book to read. As I sat down and started to read, I glanced up and noticed a very old man seated across the room. He was wrinkled and hunched over the cane he held in one hand. He looked lonely and dejected.

"Normally, I might have just smiled at him and gone back to my reading, but this time I made a conscious effort to walk over and say 'hello' to him. That's all it took. He started to talk to me. He told me about his boyhood up in Maine; he looked down at his arthritic fingers and described the tools he had made for his company which had earned him several patents. He talked about his children who were scattered across the country and hardly had time for him any more. When he spoke of his wife who had passed away twenty years ago, tears welled up in his eyes and he had to stop talking for a few moments.

"My husband returned from his business appointment after about two hours. I didn't do the reading I had intended to do, but I feel that I accomplished something much more valuable. I had shown a genuine interest in someone. I had touched another life, and to me, it had been a most beautiful experience."

Even though most members do not know each other before joining the class, and very likely will not see each other after the Course, a feeling of "togetherness" develops among them. Graduates often remark that it is the support of their classmates that helped them during the Course. As an aspect of the human relations approach, class members overcome serious problems and resolve their doubts about their inter-personal relationships. Dr. Harry Elwell, a college professor himself, who took the course in Memphis, stated it this way: "At no time did anything go outside the room. There was an empathy among the class members, however, that you could absolutely feel. It might be too loose a use of the word 'love,' but actually I believe that in a way, these people loved one another." The personal interest taken by the instructor and the close attention paid by the participants in the class make the experience much more than what one might normally ex-pect. Many skeptics who registered for the course because an employer or a family member insisted that they do so are "converted" by this deep personal involvement.

This was the experience of a Denver class member, Dan Ramsey. "The first two sessions I resisted becoming in-volved. I thought how phony can you get standing in front of all those people and telling such intimate things about your life. But after a while I really became enthusiastic and began to identify with them. These men and women were human beings and it made me project my attitudes toward them and other human beings with whom I came in con-tact. I didn't use to do that. In fact, I frankly did not like people. Since taking the course, that is all changed."

Smile is the entire statement of principle number 5. A smile is a sign of friendliness. It is the human equivalent of the dog wagging its tail. Yet, this admonition to smile has aroused more criticism of the Carnegie method than any other.

Students sometimes misinterpret this principle. It is not always applicable as there are times when a smile is not at all appropriate. A smile isn't something you put on mechani-cally as you put on a hat. A real smile is merely an outer expression of an inner condition. It is quite possible to be gracious and charming in manner without actually smiling.

And certainly, nobody outside an institution for the feeble-minded, smiles constantly.

On the other hand, there are people who rarely smile. Carnegie was frequently asked if one should force a smile even when one didn't feel like smiling. He answered that a phony smile looked just that way—phony. A smile must come from the heart. It then pushes its way outward and shows in your eyes, your voice and your actions. "Act cheerful and you'll feel cheerful."

A smile can help win over an antagonist. Sharon MacDonald, a teenager who is a volunteer in a convalescent home in Connecticut, tells of a strong, elderly patient who was creating considerable difficulties with the nurses. She refused to be treated and, short of using restraining devices on her (which they were reluctant to do), they could not keep her under control. While in a wheelchair with a tray attached to it, the patient started banging on the tray and tried to slide out from under it. She got stuck in the chair, however, and started screaming at the nurses. The nurses could not stop her and the situation degenerated into chaos. At this point, Sharon took over. She knew that the patient liked to be wheeled up and down the hall, so she went up to the chair and looking her straight in the face gave her a broad smile. The patient was startled by this sudden change from an atmosphere of conflict to the friendly approach of an attendant. She became quiet and Sharon spoke to her softly and wheeled her around. After that she allowed Sharon to feed her and administer other necessities.

Dale Carnegie summed this up: "Do you like to associate with people who are grumpy, down in the dumps and unhappy, or do you like to associate with people who are happy and radiant? Their feelings and attitudes are just as contagious as measles. So, you ought to radiate what you want other people to have.

"Remember that a person's name is the sweetest and most important sound in any language." This principle of good human relations is the very first area covered in the Dale Carnegie Course.

Once a name is learned, it should be used whenever possible. In *How to Win Friends and Influence People* Carnegie tells of an interview he had with James Farley, chairman of the Democratic Party in the 1930s. "I understand," Carnegie said, "that you can call ten thousand people by their first names." 'No, you are wrong,' he said 'I can call fifty thousand people by their first name. Make no mistake about it.' That ability helped Mr. Farley put Franklin D. Roosevelt in the White House."

Carnegie graduates often pride themselves on this ability to remember names, and report how it has helped them in business and in social life. Paul B. Corman, a business executive of Tampa, Florida, related that after he took the Course he went to a party where he met a large number of people for the first time. As he was introduced to them he repeated their names and by the end of the party he still could call three-quarters of them by name.

Another tenet of good human relations is: *Be a good listener. Encourage others to talk about themselves.* Carnegie training encourages good listening by exposing every participant to at least two talks by every student in the class. This means that students *listen* to about eighty talks each class, plus the comments of the instructor. As most of the talks are about personal experiences and feelings, each listener identifies with the speaker, and becomes aware of the importance to himself of what the speaker is saying. It conditions each student to listen, and to recognize the truth of the principle of personal identification.

A Louisville, Kentucky, class member was a successful real estate salesman. Like many successful salespeople, he liked to brag about his sales. "I used to go to the office and show off to my associates by talking about all *my* sales and *my* new listings. I guess I was rather boisterous about it and instead of regarding me as a hero, I found that my associates were resenting me. After the sessions on human relations I decided to spend more time listening to what the others had to say instead of bragging about myself. Now I ask them about *their* work and listen to *their* experiences. I was amazed at the change in their attitude toward me. They now welcome me and I look forward to listening to them."

Listening can make a big difference in one's family relations too, according to John T. Troupe of Memphis, Tennessee. "I used to come from work and kiss my wife and say 'How ya doing, Babe?' and pick up the paper and start reading and never hear what she had to say. Later in the evening I would often ask her a question and she would tell me we had already talked about that. It was pretty embarrassing. Now, by applying the rule about listening, I still say 'How ya doing, Babe?' and give her a little kiss, but I plant my feet down and stay right there and listen to what she's got to say and maybe ask a couple of questions. It has made a big difference in our lives."

In addition to developing better relationships between people, listening can also teach the listener something about the subject discussed and the person who is speaking. Terry Johnson told this story to a Dale Carnegie class in Little Rock, Arkansas:

"Last Tuesday I was in my office checking some structural steel drawings for the industrial project we are currently working on. The drawings are designs for conveyor supports, and were prepared by a young engineer in our office. Bill was very bright, but he did not have much experience in this aspect of the work. I noticed two items Bill had used, which I felt could be improved. Since my engineering registration stamp is affixed to these drawings, I have the responsibility for final decisions on the work. It is important that I agree with whatever methods are used. With this in mind I spoke to Bill to see whether I could get the two items changed to the way I thought they should be.

"I decided that the best approach in my attempt to change his mind would be to ask him questions that would get him involved in making the changes. On the first point, I had only asked two or three questions when Bill saw my point and he immediately agreed with me and we made the change on the drawing. The second item did not work out that way. I asked questions and as I heard the answers I realized that Bill's solution was better than mine. He had the problem under control and I accepted his suggestion."

Most people want someone to listen to them. Psychologists, counselors and religious leaders find that a person who has a problem is often relieved of its pressure by speaking to someone about it.

Fred Kaplan, a member of a New York City Dale Carnegie class, told how his relations with his father improved markedly. His father was always complaining and criticizing, and Fred disliked visiting him. One day when he had to accompany his father to the dentist, he decided to apply the Dale Carnegie principle number 7: *Be a good listener. Encourage others to talk about themselves.* Instead of arguing and defending himself, Fred evinced interest in what his father was saying on the way to the dentist. "When we entered the office, the waiting room was empty, except for my Dad and myself," Fred related. "About five minutes elapsed, then the miracle happened. Dad put his hand on my knee and said, 'Fred, thanks.' I answered: 'Thanks for what Dad?' He said: 'Thanks for listening to me.' Well, I was dumbfounded. Words cannot really express my feelings. I turned to him and saw tears in his eyes. He turned to me and said: 'Fred, I love you,' and we both wept."

If you want people to like you, make them feel that they are important. This Carnegie principle has paid off over and over again in interpersonal relations on the job, with friends and family, and in social situations. Everybody has something or somebody to look up to to make them feel important. As Emerson said, "Every man I meet is in some way my superior; and in that I can learn from him."

Tom Lipe, who is now a Dale Carnegie sponsor in Florida, was for many years chief of detectives of the Miami Police Department. He tells of the time a complicated case was brought to the department. "I called in John MacLendon, an old-timer, who had been with the department years before I became chief. When he came in I said to the people who were involved in the case: 'I'm assigning one of the finest detectives in this department to work on your case. If I went out myself to do this for you, I couldn't do it as well as he.' The next day Mac came into my office and said, 'Chief, I really appreciate what you said about me.' I replied: 'It's the truth. You are a better detective than I am. You've had more investigative experience.'" It was this type of thing that made it possible for these older men to accept Tom Lipe as their chief even though he was much younger and had considerably less experience on the force.

Several of the principles of human relations are closely related: *Make the other person feel important. Show respect for the other person's opinion. Appeal to the nobler motives. Give the person a fine reputation to live up to.* These principles are often applied in a combined approach.

Ronald C. Voss, a Minneapolis participant in the Dale Carnegie Course, tells of his disappointment with the C and D marks on the report card brought home by his oldest son Michael, who was really an A or B student. The teacher's comment was that Michael was not working up to his ability and had a negative attitude. Ron realized that Michael was very unhappy about his poor marks when he promised to do better next quarter. In order not to show partiality, Ron also looked into the report cards of his two other children, and found that they had satisfactory grades. On the report cards was a place for comments from parents. Ron wrote on Michael's card: "We discussed this report card with Michael and believe there will be a 100 percent improvement next quarter. My wife and I believe in Michael and are confident he will develop into a fine citizen." On each of the other children's cards we wrote: "My wife and I are proud of our child's accomplishment and believe they will continue to be a credit to your class." The next quarter's report cards showed Michael had improved: he had only one C+, and the rest were As and Bs. His attitude had also improved and he was working up to his abilities. Equally important, the grades of the two other children had also improved. By giving them an ideal to live up to, they were inspired to make the effort to achieve the higher grades.

Jim Wilson of Kalamazoo, Michigan, applied the same principle of human relations in a business situation. He had hired a bright young woman as an assistant in the art department of his company. One of the art directors with whom she would have to work was not pleased with her during the tryout period, although all the others in the art department found her work satisfactory. Jim told his class how he handled this delicate matter:

"I didn't want to force the issue by saying that he had better get used to working with her as that would have caused ill feelings between them. Instead, I used the techniques which I had learned in my Dale Carnegie classes on human relations.

"I went into his office one day and told him how much I appreciated his working long hours. I complimented him on his work and his dedication. Then I said 'You really need an assistant more than anyone else because you do so much more. If you had a young assistant who was eager to learn and advance, she wouldn't mind working hard to get ahead.'

"Then I appealed to his nobler motives by reminding him

that since he and I had more experience in the department than the others, we had a responsibility to work with young people to develop their talents. He suddenly saw himself as the wise teacher because a few days later the young lady came into my office to tell me how friendly he had become toward her, and was offering her advice on a project she was working on."

Class members are asked to speak on how they applied human relations rules in different situations. A California businessman, W. Harrison Hiatt, Jr., told of the problem he had giving orders to a man who was old enough to be his grandfather. "My job," he said, "is to see that our products are shipped. George, our shipping agent, obviously did not like taking orders from a young person. I'd keep pushing him with such comments as: 'George, let's do this; 'George, let's do that; 'George let's get this out right away.' One day he rebelled. 'I'm not in the army,' he said, 'I'm not taking any orders.' I worried about this on my way to the class. Could I apply a human relations rule to handling George? I felt the rule 'show respect for the other person's opinion' would apply. So instead of giving George orders, I began asking questions about how we might meet schedules, what we might do to service rush orders, etc. It was amazing how George changed. Not only did we have fewer difficulties on the job, but we learned to respect and even to like each other."

Another Carnegie class member, William S. Blakeman of Winchester, Kentucky, noticed one of his assistants sitting with his feet up on his desk doing absolutely nothing. Blakeman, whose own desk was piled high with work, was tempted to call him in and bawl him out for "goofing off." He reports: "Because of a pending Carnegie assignment in which I was to make the other person feel important, I decided to try a different approach. After a little small talk, I explained that all the work was ending up on my desk and that I could not get it all done. 'Do you have any ideas for improving the way we do things around here?' I asked. He offered several ideas which we discussed. Then he said, 'You know I've not had enough work to do today. Maybe I can take some of this load from you.' He had admitted he was goofing off without my having to say a word. He left determined to be more productive. I had accomplished my purpose without belittling or antagonizing him."

One of the most difficult principles for many people to accept, is: *If you are wrong, admit it quickly and emphatically.* To some people admitting a mistake connotes weakness. However, if one is wrong, acknowledging it will make the next step much easier. Good human relations must be based on honesty, and accepting one's own mistakes is the key to honest relationships.

This can be exemplified by an incident related by Mrs. Susan Simmons, a fourth-grade teacher in Sacramento, California. "One day at school," she says "I didn't feel well and was very touchy. I had warned the class that I wasn't feeling well and that they should be on their best behavior. One boy had been a regular problem and this day he really rubbed me the wrong way. I went over to him and shook him and said, 'You go out in the hall; I don't want to see you for a while.'

"Later, I realized it was my fault. I had been too touchy. I brought Ron back into the class and said: 'Children, I want to apologize to all of you for the way I flew off the handle. It was my fault—not Ron's fault. I'm very sorry and especially sorry for Ron. I'll be a bit more patient with all of you.' For the rest of the day things went better. My warning that I didn't feel well and that they should be on their best behavior was negative. Once I admitted it was my fault, not Ron's, they behaved very well. I think I was the first teacher who had ever apologized to them."

The application of this rule to a business situation has

often saved a customer for a company. Robert Peck, a manufacturer's representative for a heating, ventilating and air-conditioning company, found himself in an awkward situation. His firm was doing business with a sheet metal contractor and had some fans on order for a large building that was being constructed downtown. When the customer called for delivery, Peck's firm made an error and forgot to release the fans. When the customer did not get the fans on time, he became very upset and said he would not only refuse to do more business with this company, but would sue them for the penalty fees he would have to pay for failure to complete his assigned work on schedule. Peck let him speak and then answered: "I know you are right. You shouldn't receive this kind of treatment. You are one of our best customers. We were absolutely wrong. We made a mistake and we will do our best to correct it. I'll rent a truck, drive out to the factory and personally bring the fans back." The customer was appeased and told Peck he didn't have to make a special trip. He would do some other work on the building to avoid the penalty clause. Peck said before taking the Dale Carnegie Course and becoming aware of this human relations principle, he probably would have blown up himself, or tried to shift the blame elsewhere, or been angry at the way the customer talked to him. By admitting his error, however, he didn't lose the customer.

Every salesperson knows that to make a sale the buyer has to be induced into a receptive mood. To do this the salesperson tries to get the buyer to agree by saying "yes" to all of the preliminary questions he asks. Some people feel this is a manipulative technique. Dale Carnegie disagrees with this. In fact, the aura of approval permeates the entire Carnegie approach. When he states: "Get the other person to say 'yes, yes' immediately," he is following the principle used by Socrates in ancient Greece.

Socrates never told people they were wrong. He asked

questions with which his opponent would have to agree. He kept obtaining one admission after another until he had a whole series of yesses. Then he continued asking questions until finally, almost without realizing it, his opponent found himself reaching the conclusion Socrates had planned.

The Socratic method is used in all Carnegie teaching. The instructor works in an atmosphere of approval. He never says "no" but encourages the students by his positive approach. It works in helping the student reach a desired goal and it works when the class member applies it in interpersonal relations.

The human relations principle *Let the other person do a great deal of the talking* is another approach often used by salespeople. George Olsen, a parts manager for the W. E. Johnson Equipment Co. in Hialeah, Florida, took this very seriously. He knew he had a problem when he tried to dominate conversations and often in doing so talked himself right out of a sale. To remind him of this principle he pasted a cartoon of a "little man with the biggest set of teeth you ever saw in an equally big mouth" inside his brief case. Every time he opened the brief case, this was the first thing he saw. He reports: "At that time I was trying to sell a contract to a big firm. We visited the purchasing agent and by asking him questions and allowing him to talk, I really understood what he wanted. The fact that I let him do the greater amount of the talking and paid attention to him got me the contract."

Allan Meyers was indignant and annoyed. He had just purchased a 1973 Triumph, his first sports car, and was anxious to try it on the road. The mechanic had promised that the car would be ready on Wednesday and it was not finished. He then promised Monday delivery—and still there was no car. Allan was tempted to make a fuss and demand delivery but he remembered his Dale Carnegie teaching and started in a friendly way. He asked if there were any special problem and was told that all the parts were available, but that the mechanic, who was a volunteer policeman, had been on emergency call due to a tornado which had hit the neighboring town that weekend. The mechanic had worked all night and had had only two hours' sleep, so he had not been able to work on the car. Allan let him tell all about the tornado and the part he had played in the rescue and relief activity. He then sympathized with him and said that he understood why the car was not ready and although he would like it as soon as possible, he would not press him to rush the job. The next day Allan received a call from the mechanic to tell him the car was ready and he could have it at 5 P.M. When he picked up the car, he spoke to the mechanic for a short time, thanked him for his work and went to pay his bill.

How did he get the mechanic to do the work? The mechanic told Allan that although he had so much to do because of the days he missed while on police duty, he came in at 5:30 A.M. and started working on Allan's car, worked on it all day and went out of his way to phone him before he left his office, so he could have it that evening. Instead of pressing and demanding service, by listening to the mechanic's story, Allan had made a friend, and obtained service much faster than if he had taken a stronger approach.

Patricia Pitkin of Lakewood, Colorado, used this principle to enlist the cooperation of a senior executive for the Women's Program in her company. She knew this executive was antagonistic to the program. He had often expressed the view that a woman's place was in the home.

"When I went into his office I noticed he had several beautiful pictures hanging on his wall depicting various African scenes. I immediately commented about the pictures and he told me how he acquired them and discussed their interesting features.

"I then asked him what he liked and didn't like about the Women's Program. As he talked, I agreed with him where I could and asked questions wherever possible. I let him do most of the talking. In the course of the discussion I mentioned that I was from the 'old school' where one earned one's paycheck and did not expect anything for nothing. This started him off on the new topic and we ended the meeting twenty minutes later than planned. I could hear the buzz of his staff members waiting in the outer office for a staff meeting.

"I learned the next day that my meeting was successful. At a meeting of other directors, this executive spoke of our meeting and enlisted the support of the other managers for our Women's Program."

Dale Carnegie said that every successful person loves the game, the chance for self-expression, the chance to prove his worth, to excel, to win. So, he said, if you want to win people of spirit and ability to your way of thinking, *throw down a challenge.*

M. K. Finley, who took the Dale Carnegie Course in Poughkeepsie, New York, used this principle effectively in developing a new manager for his company. He said:

"I had an assistant manager, Bruce, who was to be trained as a manager as soon as possible, so he could be promoted into his own store. His fault was that he had difficulty finishing what he started, and consequently, many fine, creative ideas were lost. Simply telling Bruce had not solved the problem, so I asked him if he could run my store. My idea was to challenge him. If he said he couldn't I would have to find out why. If he said he could, I knew I had him because he would have to prove it.

"When I challenged him, he said he could, so I told him to manage my store for the next week. During that week he would make all decisions, but I would be around to give him advice if he needed it. "After a day, it was obvious that he could not do some of the paperwork that I had always assumed he could. The desk was a mess; papers were not filed; merchandise was not ordered; no one knew exactly what the work schedule was. Once we identified the problems they were gradually worked out and we settled into a new arrangement.

"Now, several weeks later, Bruce still runs my store. He takes care of the day-to-day operations while I am free to work on special projects. Together, we have grown in understanding of each other to the benefit of the store. When he is assigned his own store, I will miss him, but he will be able to take it over, and with full confidence become a competent manager."

It takes a great deal of courage to throw down a challenge like that and even more courage to accept it. You must have confidence in the person you so challenge, and, most important, great self-confidence in your ability to see it through.

Presenting a teen-ager with a challenge is often a way to get good results. James F. Bettle of Allentown, Pennsylvania, tells of a heart-to-heart talk he had with his daughter, Chris. "She told me that after three years of playing the clarinet in the school band she wanted to quit before the end of the semester. This came as a surprise to me because she had been enthusiastic about being in the band and the recognition it brought her. She felt that it had become boring. Chris is not a quitter and doesn't change her mind about following through on activities she undertakes. I told her the decision was up to her, and that to finish the semester would be an accomplishment in itself. I reminded her of her past accomplishments and pursuits which she carried out to satisfactory completion: she had become an accomplished horseback rider and a skilled swimmer. There was a long pause in our conversation. Then she said proudly, 'Dad, I'll stick with the band and not quit.' Chris accepted my challenge, and can live with the decision because it is hers."

How can you teach someone to be a better person? To have more effective relations with others? Obviously it is not enough to have the student memorize Dale Carnegie's twenty-one principles of good human relations. The entire Dale Carnegie philosophy of teaching is *application*. Like most of the other aspects of the Course, human relations training requires a change in attitude. It is not an area of cognitive learning which can be memorized, drilled or studied. It must be used in the daily lives of each person. To teach this requires an understanding instructor, a cooperative class member and an opportunity to test the principles in life as well as in the classroom. Very often, a class member will identify himself with someone else's problem and recognize the need for a change in attitude, or in a way of behaving, or even a major change in lifestyle and outlook.

A Utica, New York, class member told of having his eighty-year-old grandmother living with his family. She was a very independent person who liked to do things on her own. In maintaining her independence she tended to become somewhat irritable—always protesting that she could handle things by herself. "I guess what she was really saying was that she wanted some kind of love between the family and herself. I never really considered this until one of my classmates gave a talk about helping an old relative. He had applied the principle of becoming genuinely interested in this old person and really trying to understand what she desired. The class member reported that this turned their relationship around from an atmosphere of constant tension, and of worrying about hurting the older person to one of sincere friendship and love. After hearing that talk, I had to think about my own relationship with my grandmother. Since then I have spent a great deal more time with her and I feel she is much happier and I am certainly much happier."

Almost every class session brings out one or two reports from class members who wish they had applied the human relations principles to their parents when they were alive. "I never told my father how much I appreciated what he had done for me." "I never told my mother I loved her. Now it is too late."

Often, it is not too late, and lives are changed by the application of one or more of the human relations principles. Many class members tell how they made a friend of an enemy, or a better friend of an acquaintance or business associate. Jeffery Richards of Boston, Massachusetts, reported:

"On this particular morning I woke up and, as usual, rushed to get out of the house. I argued with my wife about having the house in disorder—even considering that we have two young children, ages two and three, and a dog. Apart from her, I am the only one who is housebroken. I was upset and ran out of the house. Later that day an old friend of mine came to see me at the office and told me he had just been divorced. I knew his wife and I started thinking. They had been married about the same period of time as we had. Perhaps the same problems that drove them apart would drive Eileen and me apart. Could it be that the application of those human relations principles I was learning at the Course would have saved my friend's marriage? I thought of the way I had spoken to my wife that morning and many other mornings. I thought of how I had not tried to see things as she saw them, but was impatient and appreciative of the heavy burden she had taking care of the house and two infants. So I just picked up the phone and said: 'Eileen.' 'What is it?' she asked. 'I just called to tell you I love you.' That was the turning point in our relationship."

Michael Cheung, who sponsors the Dale Carnegie Course in Hong Kong, tells of how the Chinese culture presents some special problems and how sometimes it is necessary to recognize that the benefit of applying a principle may be more advantageous than maintaining an old tradition. He had one middle-aged class member who had been estranged from his son for many years. The father had been an opium addict, but was now cured. In Chinese tradition an older person cannot take the first step. The father felt that it was up to his son to take the initiative toward a reconciliation. In an early session, his talk was about the grandchildren he had never seen and how much he desired to be reunited with his son. His classmates, all Chinese, understood his conflict between his desire and long-established tradition. The father felt that young people should have respect for their elders and that he was right in not giving in to his desire, but to wait for his son to come to him.

Toward the end of the Course the father made his human relations talk. "I have pondered this problem," he said. "Dale Carnegie says, 'if you are wrong, admit it quickly and emphatically.' It is too late for me to admit it quickly but I can admit it emphatically. I wronged my son. He was right in not wanting to see me and to expel me from his life. I may lose face by asking a younger person's forgiveness, but I was at fault and it is my responsibility to admit this." The class applauded and gave him their full support. At the next class he told how he went to his son's house, asked for and received forgiveness and was now embarked on a new relationship with his son, his daughter-in-law and the grandchildren he had at last met.

A San Carlos, California, class member indicated in the first session that he wanted to become a better communicator and be able to speak more effectively before groups. His manner and style of speaking, and the apparent self-confidence he had right from the beginning made the instructor feel there was something deeper than this man sought. After a few sessions, the class member had a sudden insight. "I thought my problem was communicating, and it was. However, it did not come from my inability to speak, but my inability to listen. While in the classroom I was forced to listen to what others had to say. Instead of my usual habit of letting what people say go in one ear and out the other, I began to really listen. I also think I learned by watching the instructor. He took a sincere interest in each person. I tried to pick up some of his techniques and saw that it wasn't a trick or gimmick. He was sincerely interested in what each person was saying, and this made all of us feel for and with him. I now put this insight into effect in my own life and it has certainly made a big difference in the way other people react to me."

A good many class members have gained greater insights into themselves without any help from instructors. They acquire these insights by thinking of those aspects of their lives on which they are going to talk. Still others go to the instructor or a graduate assistant for help in formulating their thinking.

Most class members are not "problem people." They are average men and women who want to improve themselves. They are successful in most areas of their lives, but they take the course to make themselves more successful.

"I was a successful salesman long before I took the Dale Carnegie Course," said Donald M. Fordyce, of New York City. "My problem was that I was too demanding of people who worked for me. I couldn't keep a staff because somehow I antagonized everyone, from the clerks in the office to salespeople under my management. Fortunately, I recognized that this was hindering my development. I wanted more success than I could achieve alone. You have to have people work with you, or you will never get into top management. By applying the rules of human relations I now have people supporting me instead of putting roadblocks in my way. At the age of thirty-five I became president of my company."

Every class member is given a wallet-sized booklet, *The Golden Book,* which lists the basic tenets of Carnegie teaching. They are drawn from *How to Win Friends and Influence People* and *How to Stop Worrying and Start Living.* Graduates often carry this book with them and frequently refer to it. Many have written for copies to replace those lost or damaged that they had been carrying with them for years. Dog-eared *Golden Books* are pulled out of wallets or purses day after day, year after year, by graduates to refresh their memory of a principle or just reinspire them with the Dale Carnegie spirit.

Salespeople are seen reading the booklet in buyers' offices while awaiting appointments. One salesperson said that whether he had a five-minute or a fifty-minute wait, going over *The Golden Book* would set him up properly for the meeting. "I really could quote it from memory," he said, "but reading it psychs me up for the meeting."

Paul Gorman of Tampa, Florida, finds *The Golden Book* handy as a reminder to follow the precepts. "One of the greatest things that helped me was remembering to talk in terms of the other person's interest. Like most people, I tend to talk about the things that interest me. So I underlined that principle in my *Golden Book* and every time I open it, it cautions me to apply it. Instead of taking six months to get to know somebody I now can accomplish this right away."

Phil Deane, now a Carnegie sponsor in Knoxville, Tennessee, organized the first classes in Venezuela. As there were no trained instructors who could conduct the classes in Spanish, those early classes were limited to people who spoke English. Most of them were Americans or Britons living in that country. Following the usual practice, the students were invited to bring a guest with them at the first session. One of the students, Hedley ("Scotty") Scott brought his wife, Helen. "When she got up to tell her name in the first part of the session," Deane tells, "I was very impressed by her beautiful speaking voice. I was sure she didn't need a class in speaking and would probably not enroll. However, she did join the class and took an active part in every session. At the final session she started her talk by saying, 'Thank

God for the Dale Carnegie Course.' I thought it was a little dramatic. She continued, 'The course has made me a better person, a better wife, a better mother and a better neighbor.' "

Dale Carnegie did not promise magic improvements in human relations skills. His successors in teaching the Course make no guarantees that by applying the Carnegie principle one will automatically become a better person and have a happier life.

There are some who have taken the Course and yet continue in their old habits and gain nothing from the training. Only those who make an effort to apply what is offered in the sessions find that it really works. Dale Carnegie admitted that the rules do not always solve one's problems. He said he was sorry he never got around to writing what he had planned as a last chapter in *How to Win Friends and Influence People*. He intended to say that "there are times when none of the rules will work and you have to throw them out of the window. Somebody has to go to jail, be spanked, divorced, knocked down, sued in court. The basic rule is to respect the right of everybody to good treatment, but sometimes you come across people who won't let you treat them that way. Then it is time for direct action, a trip to the woodshed perhaps. There are times when courteous treatment is not good human relations; if you are attacked, there may be no answer but self-defense and self-preservation." However, by applying the principles of good human relations, these situations will be minimized. Preventive maintenance keeps a machine from breaking down; preventive maintenance in human relations keeps this important phase of life tuned up and prevents breakdowns in one's dealings with family, friends, co-workers and all of those people with whom we interact in our daily lives.

7

Applying the Human Factor to Business

By thinking the right thoughts, you can make any job less distasteful. Your boss wants you to be interested in your job so that he will make more money. But let's forget what the boss wants. Remind yourself that it may double the amount of happiness you get out of life, for you spend about one-half of your waking hours at your work, and if you don't find happiness in your work, you many never find it anywhere. Keep reminding yourself that getting interested in your job will take your mind off your worries, and, in the long run, will probably bring promotion and increased pay. Even if it doesn't do that, it will reduce fatigue to a minimum and help you enjoy your hours of leisure. —DALE CARNEGIE

Human relations skills are the foundations of good management. To translate Dale Carnegie principles of human relations into managerial ability, a special program was developed—The Dale Carnegie Management Seminar. This course was originally created as a program for managers and licensed sponsors in the Carnegie organization. It was so successful in building management skills within the organization that it was offered to the public in 1967. Since then, more than forty thousand people have taken this seminar in the United States, Japan, Brazil, Spain, Germany, Australia, New Zealand, Canada, Argentina, Iceland, England, France, Switzerland, Denmark, Hong Kong and many other countries.

On the evening of June 20, 1972, twenty-three executives of the Piper Aircraft Corporation, the manufacturer of the famous "Piper Cub" and other small aircraft, completed their last session of the Management Seminar. Outside, strong gusts of wind were blowing. The seminar leader cut short the graduation ceremonies so that the participants could leave before the storm reached its height. It was the onset of Hurricane Agnes, one of the worst disasters to strike the eastern part of the United States.

When the storm was over the area hit was in shambles— $1.7 billion dollars worth of property was damaged and 134 people were dead. The Piper factory was in ruins. $23 million in planes, inventory, buildings and equipment were destroyed. Assembly lines lay under several feet of water. Aircraft damaged by the flood were unsalvageable. Warehouse and assembly inventory were caked with mud. Tools, files, supplies were either missing or ruined beyond repair.

J. M. Mergen, president of the company, and his staff gloomily surveyed the ruins. "It was almost a complete disaster," he said, "but once we recovered from the initial shock, my people decided to rebuild and get us back into production as fast as possible. Our most optimistic estimate was that we would not be able to resume production and deliver new planes until December at the earliest."

As the management team had just completed the Management Seminar, they began to apply the principles they had learned to rebuilding the company. A careful estimate of the situation was made. Department by department the company was examined to determine what had to be done, and goals and time-tables were set up in each division and department.

The plans were broken into "bite-sized" pieces and everybody was informed what the goals and sub-goals were.

Findley Estlick, vice president and general manager of the Lock Haven Division, said: "Using the management techniques taught in the Carnegie seminar, we conducted meetings with our supervisors and quickly received thirty or forty constructive suggestions, and these served as a basis for the reorganization."

John R. Piper, production engineering manager, reported: "Everybody was encouraged to participate. Goals were set, and because we operated in a goal-oriented environment, all our people became involved. They related their activities to the total picture and responded with greater enthusiasm and cooperation because the entire program was their program.

Each manager worked closely with subordinates, delegating whatever could be delegated, analyzing problems systematically as they arose and making decisions at the operational level wherever possible. Despite the almost insurmountable problems, morale was high. Everyone contributed his or her best to the rebuilding of the facilities."

President Mergen summed up the result: "There was quick, effective communication between people at every level. A high degree of teamwork, motivation and personal involvement by everyone was generated. Because of the greater cooperation between divisions and departments which was set in motion by the seminar, we started delivering new airplanes in September—*three months ahead of the original estimate.*"

Like all Carnegie courses the Management Seminar is a participating seminar. Those attending come from all ranks of management and from all types of organizations, including manufacturing companies, banks, retail establishments, hospitals, school districts, government agencies and non-profit organizations. Some organizations send their entire management team to a seminar and others, like Piper, have special in-house seminars run for them.

The emphasis of the seminar is that management involves *managing through people.* It stresses that success is achieved by enlisting the willing cooperation of people to reach desired goals. The manager is shown how this can be accomplished using the primary functions of management: planning, organizing, directing, coordinating and controlling; and the personal skills that one can develop in management: creative thinking, motivation, delegation, problem analysis and decision making and communicating.

Among the objectives of the management seminars is encouraging participants to develop and use creative thinking in solving problems. This is done by means of brainstorming or green-light thinking sessions, in which class members are given the opportunity to work on problems creatively right there in the class. As a corollary, each participant is advised, and indeed is required, to engage in some personal project after each session, to enhance effectiveness on the job and to save or make money for the organization.

One class member who worked for a large public utility thought about what he could do to save money for his company. When he left the seminar that evening he opened his car trunk to store his briefcase and other papers and noticed the spare tire. He reported to the class at the next session: "I stared at that tire and although I must have seen it a thousand times, it suddenly occured to me that here was a superfluous item. According to company rules, if a company car had a flat tire, the driver was not allowed to touch it. The garage had to be notified and a mechanic was sent to change it. Our company had a fleet of several hundred cars. We purchased all of them with spare tires. By eliminating the fifth wheel, we could save a considerable amount of money. The mechanic could bring along the extra wheel when needed." An innovative approach to a routine situation saved this company thousands of dollars over the years.

The key to higher productivity is often good planning followed by effective controls. Seminar participants are asked to set up a one-year plan for themselves and to establish a positive control system to assure success for the plan.

Probably the most significant change that occurs among participants is in their attitude toward people. Supervisors and managers are encouraged to give their people more responsibility and the authority to carry out their jobs. They are taught to communicate with their subordinates and to help them grow by allowing them to use their own abilities and strengths to solve problems, and not to bother the boss with them.

Alan Beatty, vice president of finance for Recreation Product Group, Victor Comptometer Corporation, summed up his reaction to the seminar: "I noticed more confidence in the attitude of the people who took the program. They were willing to attack problems rather than brush them under the rug. They were more willing to talk about problems. I also think they were a little more understanding of the new people they hired and a little more helpful in training them and communicating with them and motivating them."

At the core of the seminar, as in other Carnegie courses, is the development of self-confidence. A manager without self-confidence cannot delegate, cannot communicate, cannot motivate. By developing the skills in these and other areas, the confidence of the participant is reinforced.

This was well expressed by Charles T. Thompson, president of a New Jersey manufacturing firm: "Most significant is the amount of self-confidence that this course instilled in a number of the individuals who attended it. The recognition that each of these people has had from those in charge of the company's program, is, to a large extent, due to the realization that others in the business have similar problems. Recognizing that everybody has shortcomings, they were able to overcome their own by applying the principles of the seminar."

As in all the other Dale Carnegie courses, communication skills are taught in the Management Seminar. Charles Thompson stated: "One of the greater contributions the seminar had provided our company is that of opening up the communication channels and placing each one of these managers on what they assume to be an equal basis with regard to experience and competence. They are more inclined to ask questions without embarrassment and to make contributions without fear of any form of recrimination. As a result, we have been able to process a restructuring plan to full execution in a fraction of the time required in previous years. This has occurred because our managers have a better understanding of the management process and its needs."

Managing one's own time and that of subordinates is one of the chief ingredients of success in management. The seminar includes a time-management exercise which had made many participants more productive. Doris Elfman, secretary-treasurer of Home Security Consultants, Inc., of New York City, used the time-management system to study what her staff was actually doing with their workdays over a period of time and was able to rearrange the work loads for a more equitable and productive distribution. She also examined her own use of time and by eliminating, combining or delegating some of her work, she freed herself for more creative and higher level activities.

Participants in the seminar come from all types of businesses and organizations. A typical public class might include a president of a small company, a plant manager and some of the foremen from a division of a major corporation, the vice president of a bank and two assistant vice presidents, a director of nursing, and some supervisory nurses from a local hospital, an officer of the Salvation Army, and the principal of a high school.

A recent class in New York City included an official of the United Nations, an administrator of a senior citizens' residence, an executive of the Boy Scouts of America, the training director of a major oil company, and a variety of business managers.

The interaction among this diverse group gave each a better understanding of problems faced in organizations so different from their own. They recognized the universal character of management problems. "We all deal with people," Jim Martin, an executive of a life insurance company, commented. "People problems are much the same whether we are out to make a profit or run a community service."

Joan Jefferson, a training specialist for a drug rehabilitation program in Harlem, reported: "When I took this course, management techniques were not being used in a consistent or a widespread way within nonprofit organizations that existed in poor communities, and were headed and staffed by community people. By applying these principles in my unit, I was able to make this unit function. I was a new and basically untrained manager and the knowledge and application of this information I acquired in the seminar was invaluable."

The Dale Carnegie Sales Course enhances the ability to communicate. Like all Carnegie courses, it is pragmatic—low on theory and high on application.

The objectives of this course are: providing practical knowledge of the sales process and thereby developing selling skills. These skills are developed on a continuing basis, through application to day-to-day selling. Emphasis is on motivational selling, time management, setting and achieving of goals, attitude control and the development of greater enthusiasm.

Percy Whiting's book, *The Five Great Rules of Selling,* is used as the text in the course. The application of these rules and the other techniques of salesmanship is reinforced at each meeting when the students report on how they applied them during the preceding week. Results are often shown immediately. After his first session, A. Rockford, an Illinois salesman, wrote to his instructor: "I have only been a student for the first session, but the one thing you said was 'Give your prospect enough facts about your product and how it will benefit him so he is justified in buying.' It works like a charm. I wrote an order today, one day after the class.

It will amount to $16,000. All I can say is THANKS and see you in class next week."

A Philadelphia class member, Anthony M. Mirabile, who sells pump packing material for Sellers Process Equipment Company, reported on how he used the fact-bridge-benefit technique with a customer. This technique involves showing the customer how the assets of the product actually will solve problems the customer faces—an exercise in better communication.

"The product that I was trying to sell was called Ramilon and sold for twenty-five dollars per pound. The competitive product that they were using cost six dollars per pound. My benefits included less downtime and less maintenance cost because our product lasted much longer.

"I had to justify the much higher cost. By working closely with the director of purchasing, I was able to calculate that, because of less downtime and maintenance, they would actually save seven hundred dollars for every twenty-five dollars they spent. I not only obtained the order, but have had several new orders since and have been asked to talk about pump packing to the local plant engineers' club."

Mirabile obtained his sale by applying the principles of good salesmanship. He dramatized the benefits by calculating the exact savings rather than by just stating that there would be less downtime and maintenance cost.

One of the highlights of the Sales Course is the discussion of buying signals—those little hints a customer gives that indicates to an astute salesperson that there is real interest. This is done in the class by skits put on by the group leaders (course graduates who assist the instructors). Lynn Hamilton, a sales representative for National Car Rental System in Pittsburgh, indicated that she was so often involved in her own presentation that she failed to notice these buying signals. The course alerted her to watch for them and to take action.

Miss Hamilton stated: "Previously, before taking the course, I would go on a sales call and would talk about my product and my service and not really ask enough questions to find out exactly what the customer was interested in. I knew what I wanted to say and said it without considering the customer at all. Now I am always concerned with the customer's interests and dominant buying motive. I waste less time and get much further with my customers."

To bring the principles of human relations to people who deal with the public, the Carnegie organization offers a Customer Relations Course. Among those who take these courses are retail salespeople, telephone salespeople, repair and service personnel and others who do not sell directly to customers but must relate to them on the job.

The basic theme of the Dale Carnegie Customer Relations Course is that the average individual sincerely wants his or her services to be valued and appreciated, but is often unaware or insensitive to the needs and attitudes of customers.

A group of forty station attendants from the New Jersey Gasoline Retailers' Association listened intently as the Dale Carnegie Customer Relations Course instructor told this incident:

"I drove into the station and the attendant slowly ambled over to my car. He muttered something that sounded like 'How many?' After he filled the tank and I paid him, he walked off without even a 'thank you.'

"Would you go back to that station? The refiners spend millions of dollars advertising for customers to buy their brands. The owner of the station spends thousands more to bring people into the stations and the attendant drives them away by the way he treats the customer.

"If you invited somebody to your home, how would you greet them? Would you have them wait at the door for five minutes after they rang the bell? Would you open the door and mutter some vague remark? Or would you welcome them into your home? And when they left would you let them go without saying goodbye?

"Customers coming into your station are just like guests coming into your home. You welcome them, thank them for coming and assure them they are welcome back."

Norman Sisisky, president of the Pepsi-Cola Bottling Company of Petersburg, Va., found that calling a customer by name increased the productivity of his route salespeople. "Dale Carnegie's principle of human relations: 'Remember that a person's name is to that person the sweetest and most important sound in any language' had a great effect on these salespeople and by practicing it they improved their customer relations.

This point was stressed in the Dale Carnegie Customer Relations Course conducted for the New Jersey Gasoline Dealers' Association. "The station attendant who remembers and uses the names of customers will develop repeat customers. A driver will pass by a gas station with a price a few cents lower than yours to patronize a place where he or she is known, greeted by name and welcomed."

A number of banks and savings and loan associations use the Dale Carnegie Customer Relations Course for tellers and others who deal with their customers. Although these people are not selling anything, they are in constant contact with customers and their attitudes and actions can affect the image of the banks and the savings and loan associations in the community.

The executive vice president of a savings and loan association in Illinois had this to say about the graduates of the Dale Carnegie Customer Relations Course in his organization: "They enjoy their work more. They've got that smile for the customer. It's a natural smile because they realize that they are sincerely interested in the customer. They are not afraid of any question that is asked of them even if they can't answer it. They know whom to turn to. They have also improved their ability to communicate with both the customer and their fellow workers in the organization. They have become better listeners and as a result are able to respond more positively and more effectively.

"You just can't tell people to give service unless they are motivated to do so. We've got to help them develop. We compete for customers just like any other savings and loan association. We cannot offer higher rates than others because the rates are regulated by government. But the one thing I think we can do to beat the competition is offer better service. The only way we can do this is to properly train our people. The Dale Carnegie Customer Relations Course was a big step in that direction."

The Heironimus Department Store in Roanoke, Virginia, has sent most of its sales personnel to the Dale Carnegie Customer Relations Course. When a class completed the course, Heironimus ran an advertisement in the local paper showing a photo of the graduates with an explanation of the course. A typical ad run in May 1972 read:

HERE COME THE PROFESSIONAL PEOPLE PLEASERS
They're our honor students. Graduates of the third Dale Carnegie Customer Relations Course. You'll know them by their sincere smile, warm, friendly attitude and their genuine effort to help you when you shop Heironimus. Our success depends on your happiness and pleasing you is our goal in training our salespeople . . .

The president of an Arkansas bank indicated that the bank's customers commented on the friendly atmosphere in the bank and the attitude of the employees since they took the Dale Carnegie Customer Relations Course.

In a letter to Leo Hawkins, sponsor in Arkansas, he wrote: "Since the beginning of the course, the number of new accounts opened in the various departments of the bank increased almost 94 percent. This is due to the fact that many of our employees who felt they did not have the ability to sell the various services of the bank are now our top salespeople."

The Dale Carnegie Personnel Development Course is similar to the Dale Carnegie Customer Relations Course, but the emphasis is on dealing with the public and fellow employees rather than with customers. Companies use this program to train potential supervisors in how to deal with people and so earn advancement. The course is also used to train administrative personnel who work closely with others within the organization, or with vendors, government regulating agencies and the community.

The core of this program is the development of good human relations and effective communication. Among the subjects covered are: how to make the job more interesting, fashioning attitudes that make the days more productive, understanding oneself and others, using self-direction and goal setting, generating enthusiasm for better self-expression, how to ask pertinent questions, how to listen more effectively, and how to cope with change.

Dale Carnegie Personnel Development Courses have been given to all kinds of organizations including government agencies, automobile dealerships, factories and banks.

The vice president of an auto dealership in Pompano Beach, Florida, found that this course trained their people to get along better with each other. "For example," he writes, "a common problem in our business is that the mechanic has to go to the Parts Department to ask for a part, and many times has a long wait. Prior to the Dale Carnegie Personnel Development Course, tempers sometimes flared in this situation. However, since the training, we found that the new attitudes and insights gained helped stop this situation."

One of the highlights of the Dale Carnegie Personnel Development Course covers the handling of complaints. Four steps are suggested:

Respect the person making the complaint. To him or her this is an important matter about which they are unhappy.

Listen. Let the person tell the whole story without interrupting.

Show appreciation. "I appreciate your bringing this to my attention."

Apologize for any inconvenience the problem may have caused.

Marvin Webber, executive vice president of the Illinois National Bank of Rockford, Illinois, reported that in the week after the session on handling complaints, a customer came into his office terribly upset about some policy of the bank's. Webber used the steps he had learned the week before, but it did no good. The customer was still angry and closed out his accounts.

A few weeks later he returned to the bank and apologized to Webber. He said he had been wrong and he appreciated the way Webber had handled the situation. He not only reopened the accounts he had closed, but added a new substantial account.

Another banker, Peter C. Haas, assistant vice president of the First National State Bank of Central New Jersey, wrote to Marilyn Westrom, a Carnegie representative: "The session on dealing with complainers was of prime importance to us and I think we all learned to be a little more tolerant of a dissatisfied customer."

Some people believe that practicing Dale Carnegie principles even if they do not really believe in them, may help to get them a sale or to influence someone. They have missed the point Carnegie was trying to make and they do an injustice to the philosophy of the Course.

Dorothy Carnegie emphasized this when she said: "Human relations has nothing to do with liking and being liked by people. If I thought that was the point of what we were doing, I'd quit and sell out tomorrow. Human relations is communication between people. It is a modern way to express the Golden Rule. It is a recognition of individuals, not just a mass of statistics on how one person scored over another by practicing certain tricks designed to give an impression of good will where there was none.

"Human relations is the essence of civilized society. It is recognizing the importance of the individual. You don't have to love a person to get along with him or her, but you must recognize other human beings as you want them to recognize you and accord them the same rights you are entitled to as a human being. Treat them with justice and acknowledge their drives, and forgive their mistakes as you expect them to forgive yours.

"As far as liking people and being liked by others goes, that is something most people cannot control. But we can control the way we treat people, and everyone is entitled to good treatment. It has nothing to do with calling a person by his first name and clapping his back. You can even fight with a person and have good human relations with him or her. Sometimes people need to be challenged and fought.

"One reason for the tremendous success of our Dale Carnegie Course is our insistence on the importance of the individual. We work entirely on this fundamental principle, that all of us are different from one another, and that difference must be recognized and respected. Everyone has this vital core of individuality; it is up to us to help remove the wraps that swathe it so that it can shine out and be free to operate. When that happens, a person is communicating his thoughts, feelings and ideas to others in his own highly personal and distinctive style. It is a great release of energy, strength and resources of personality which may have lain dormant and untapped."

8

Conquering Worry

Am I advocating that we simply bow down to all the adversities that come our way? Not by a long shot! That is mere fatalism. As long as there is a chance that we can save a situation, let's fight! But when common sense tells us that we are up against something that is so—and cannot be otherwise— then in the name of our sanity, let's not "look before and after and pine for what is not." —DALE CARNEGIE

How can a course in effective speaking and human relations help a person conquer worry? In the early days of the Course, Dale Carnegie noted that many of the class members' talks centered around their own fears and worries. In his book *How to Stop Worrying and Start Living* which resulted from this observation, Carnegie wrote:[1]

"A large majority of my students were businessmen: executives, salesmen, engineers, accountants, a cross section of all the trades and professions, and most of them had problems! There were women in the classes—businesswomen and housewives. They, too, had problems! Clearly, what I needed was a textbook on how to conquer worry—so again I tried to find one. I went to the New York Public Library and discovered to my astonishment that even this excellent library had only twenty-two books listed under the title WORRY. I also noticed, to my amusement, that it had 189 books listed under WORMS. *Almost nine times as many books about worms as worry!* Astounding, isn't it? Since worry is one of the biggest problems facing mankind, you would think, wouldn't you, that every high school and college in the land

[1] Dale Carnegie, *How to Stop Worrying and Start Living* (New York: Simon and Schuster, 1948), pp. xiii–xiv.

would give a course on 'How to Stop Worrying?' Yet, if there is even one course on that subject in any college in the land, I have never heard of it. No wonder David Seabury said in his book *How to Worry Successfully:* 'We come to maturity with as little preparation for the pressures of experience as a bookworm asked to do a ballet.'

"The result? More than half of our hospital beds are occupied by people with nervous and emotional troubles.

"I looked over these twenty-two books on worry reposing on the shelves of the New York Public Library. In addition, I purchased all the books on worry I could find; yet I couldn't discover even one that I could use as a text in my course for adults. So I resolved to write one myself."

Dale Carnegie and his staff interviewed scores of people on how they overcame worry. They read biographies of famous people who had faced serious problems and learned how they overcame them.

"I also did something that was far more important than the interviewing and the reading. I worked for five years in a laboratory for conquering worry—a laboratory conducted in our own adult classes. As far as I know, it was the first and only laboratory of its kind in the world. This is what we did: We gave the students a set of rules on how to stop worrying and asked them to apply these rules in their own lives and then to talk to the class on the results they had obtained. Others reported on techniques they had used in the past.

"As a result of this experience, I presume I have listened to more talks on "How I Conquered Worry" than has any other individual who has ever walked this earth. In addition, I *read* hundreds of other talks on "How I Conquered Worry'— talks that were sent to me by mail—talks that won prizes in our classes throughout the United States and Canada. . . ."

These talks still are a basic part of the Dale Carnegie Course. Class members are given copies of Carnegie's book *How to Stop Worrying and Start Living* when they start the

Course and begin to absorb the suggestions it contains. Later in the Course, they report on how they applied these principles. Many of these talks reflect significant changes in the lives of the speakers as a result of Carnegie's teachings. More important, however, is the inspiration each talk gives others in the class. Ideas which they had read and accepted intellectually, but had not emotionally become real to them are clarified when they hear how they had benefited their classmates. In the final meeting of the class, many students report on how a talk at the session on worry had given them the courage to apply the Carnegie concepts in their own lives and had helped them overcome fears which had plagued them for years.

Let us look at some of these principles and how they were put into practice by Carnegie class members.

Dale Carnegie's first rule is: *Live in Day-Tight Compartments.* He tells of the famous surgeon, William Osler, who compared life to the modern ocean liner in which the captain can seal off various parts of the ship into watertight compartments. Osler carried this forward. "What I urge is that you so learn to control the machinery (of your life) as to live with *day-tight compartments* as the most certain way to insure safety on the voyage. Touch a button and hear, at every level of your life, the iron doors shutting out the past—the dead yesterdays. . . . Touch another and shut off, with a metal curtain, the future, the unborn tomorrows. . . . Shut off the past! Let the dead past bury its dead. . . . Shut out the yesterdays that have lighted fools the way to dusty death. . . . Shut off the future as tightly as the past. The future is today . . . waste of energy, mental distress, nervous worries dog the steps of the man who is anxious about the future. . . . Shut close, then, the great fore and aft bulkheads, and prepare to cultivate the habit of life in *day-tight compartments.*"

Dale Carnegie goes on to assure us that Osler did not mean we should not prepare for tomorrow, but that the best way to prepare for tomorrow is to concentrate on doing today's work today. The great Roman poet, Horace, agreed. He wrote:

> Happy the man and happy he alone,
> He who can call today his own,
> He who, secure within can say,
> Tomorrow, do thy worst
> For I have lived today.

Almost every class brings out talks in which the students tell of being worried—often to the point of nervous exhaustion—about something that happened months or even years ago. Mrs. Victoria MacNamara of Fort Lauderdale, Florida, told how her life was haunted by the memory of a wrong she had done to a person, now dead. She would wake up in the middle of the night in a sweat and be unable to get back to sleep. During the day her thoughts would suddenly revert to this alleged wrong. She reported: "It was not easy to put this out of my mind and it still comes back from time to time. However, I now close those day-tight compartments and think of today's problems and joys. I am gradually learning to let the dead past bury its dead."

James Feiler, president of a cabinet-making contracting business in San Francisco, also had trouble sleeping. "Being a business executive, especially in your own business, there is a tendency to take it to bed with you at night. Since taking the Course I have been following Dale Carnegie's advice. I feel I have done the best I could each day and to lie there and worry about what will happen tomorrow is only going to put me in a position where tomorrow I'm not going to be half as good as I could be if I had a good night's sleep. I shut out the next day until it arrives and I sleep much better than I ever did before and feel better the next day."

Unexpected responsibilities thrust upon Robert Baran changed him from a happy person to a worrier. When his boss had a sudden massive coronary, he had to take full charge of his department. He reported: "At first there was confusion. Then, total chaos. My boss had been the type of man who kept everything in his head and only gave you enough information to enable you to struggle along in a job. Then came worry. I worried that I wouldn't be able to fulfill a supervisor's role. I worried about the mountain of work that was piling up higher and higher each day and I hadn't the faintest idea as to what to approach first. I worried whether my fellow employees would change their attitude about me now that I was their boss. But worst of all, I didn't stop my worrying after hours. I took it home with me. I spent sleepless nights of tossing and turning only to face another day of seemingly endless tasks.

"Approximately three months after being thrown into this lion's den, I enrolled in the Dale Carnegie Course. One afternoon I picked up his book *How to Stop Worrying and Start Living*. As I kept reading, I suddenly began to realize how foolish I had been. I realized that despite all the worrying I had been doing, the job was being done effectively—often with praise from my superiors. How foolish I had been to worry so much. From that day on I vowed to take one day at a time and live in 'day-tight compartments.' And you know what? It works!

"I was particularly impressed by some of the maxims Dale Carnegie quoted such as 'Today is the tomorrow you worried about yesterday.' So I sat down and started concentrating on the word "worry' and came up with his acronym which I printed and have mounted on the wall next to my desk":

> W orry
> O nly
> R educes the
> R esources within
> Y ou.

A Carnegie class member in Gambier, Ohio, Kimberly Bergs was moved to write the following poem as a result of her study of these principles:

LIVING

Life is too short
To live in the past
For the present and future
Are leaving us fast.
Worry not that your past
Will with you remain
For then in your future
There's nothing to gain.
Live life to the fullest,
And live it each day;
Worry not for the future
And forget yesterday.
For yesterday is gone,
But today is brand new,
And if you live it as much,
Fresh new things you'll do.
Each day is alive
With new hopes and despairs,
But don't dwell on either,
For they soon are not there.
For the past was the present
and the present will pass,
And the future is coming,
But it passes too fast.
So live for today
And tomorrow will come.
Live life to the fullest
For it too soon is done.

Perhaps the most quoted of Carnegie's principles of conquering worry is his three-step formula:

Step 1: Ask yourself what is the worst that can possibly happen.
Step 2: Prepare to accept it if you have to.
Step 3: Then calmly proceed to improve on the worst.

Duncan Ehlers, a Carnegie careerist, was introduced to the world of Dale Carnegie through the use of this formula. In his own words: "It was shortly after World War II. I had returned to England after a long stay in Argentina and was in a very boring job. It was keeping cost records for the large conglomerate in which all members of our family worked. I was constantly worried. The work was dull. I was afraid I'd be stuck there forever. I worried I might disgrace my family by being fired. I worried I would never make a success of my life. I began to get stomach pains which stayed with me all the time. My doctor prescribed some medicine, but it didn't help. The only time the pains disappeared was over the weekends when I wasn't at work. They returned on Mondays as I started back to the office.

"Some weeks later, while browsing in a bookstore I came across Dale Carnegie's *How to Stop Worrying and Start Living.* When I reached Chapter 2 in which the 'magic formula' is given, I decided right then to apply it to my situation.

"What was the worst that could happen? It was unlikely I'd be fired. Big companies rarely fire anyone, but I could be stuck in this boring job for years.

"Prepare to accept it if you have to. My first thought was that I had to accept this because it was a secure job, but the second part of the rule 'if you have to' soon dominated my thoughts.

"Calmly prepare to improve on the worst. I could improve on my situation by asking for a transfer. This might seem an obvious answer today, but back then it was unheard of for a junior person to ask for a transfer. Such action had to be initiated by higher management. However, I felt I could not

continue as I was, so the next day I requested an interview with one of the top men in the company. The result—a transfer to a much more interesting job in South America.

"Incidentally, once I left the dull job, the pain in my stomach disappeared and it has never come back."

The use of this magic formula has had some interesting repercussions. When New York City was faced with one of its recurring financial crises, it was compelled to lay off a number of civil service employees, some with considerable seniority. Most of these people had considered a city job totally secure and the prospect of unemployment was traumatic.

One of these men, William J. Borchers, a city fireman, was particularly worried. He was in that in-between area—not quite sure if he had enough seniority to be safe. The cutoff point might be above or below this level. He worried about what he would do if he lost his job and yet there was an even chance that he would not be laid off.

Applying the magic formula helped overcome this constant worry. The worst that could happen: he would lose his job. He could accept that. He was still young. He could restructure his life. What could he do about it now? He decided to go back to school and prepare for a new career. Once the decision was made, the worry no longer dominated his life. Even if he were retained on the job, he would pursue his education. This would help him if a later layoff caught up with him or when he retired or decided to leave the fire department.

Vincent Raab, who took the Course in Garden City, New York, applied a four-step adaptation of this formula to a problem he had. Raab, an accountant with a hospital on Long Island, had set up a more efficient payroll system but ran into an argument with the chief of one of the medical services concerning the new system. The doctor complained to the hospital director about him. Raab had observed that the director usually would support a medical doctor in a dispute with an administrator and was worried about the repercussions of this argument.

(1) What am I worried about? Being fired or at least reprimanded.
(2) What can I do about it? One alternative was to hope it would be ignored by the hospital director. Another was to apologize to the doctor and allow him to ignore the new system. A third alternative was to bring the matter to the director of finance, his immediate boss.
(3) Decide what to do. Raab chose to bring this to the attention of his boss.
(4) When? Immediately. The next morning he discussed the entire matter with the director of finance, who backed him fully. The hospital director agreed he was right.

By applying this formula, Raab was able to solve his problem and at the same time alleviate hours (or maybe days) of unnecessary worry.

When Margaret Cooney of Towson, Maryland, woke up one morning to discover that her newly finished basement was flooded, she almost panicked. "My first impulse," she reported "was to sit down and cry and feel sorry for myself. Instead I asked myself what is the worst thing that can happen? The answers were easy: the furniture could be ruined; the paneling could warp and be left with watermarks; the carpet could be ruined, and our insurance might not cover any of it.

"Next, I asked myself what I could do to reduce the chance of having all of these things happen. I asked the kids to begin carrying out all of the portable furniture to the garage, which was dry. I reported the damage to the insurance agent and then called carpet cleaners to come with a water vacuum. I washed the machine washable items, such as the pillows. Then the children and I borrowed extra dehumidifiers from the neighbors to help speed the drying process. By the time my husband came home, things were under control.

"The lesson I learned from my Dale Carnegie training worked well here. I considered the worst that could happen, figured out how to reduce the chances of that happening and then *got busy* and did what had to be done. I had no time to worry."

Worry causes more illnesses than many organic problems. Some doctors claim that more than half of all hospital patients are ill because of worry or have their ailments worsen because of worry. Yet many of the things we worry about will look ridiculous when the immediate concern is over. Many worries concern trivialities. Even a few hours later we wonder why we were so upset. A well-known legal maxim says: *De minimus non curat lex. The law does not concern itself with trifles.* Neither should the worrier, if the worrier wants peace of mind.

Not only do people worry unnecessarily about trifles, but they worry about things that probably will never happen. People worry about diseases they are not likely to get, accidents that will probably not happen, business problems that may occur once in a thousand transactions, and countless other matters. If we could look at the statistical chances of something we are worried about actually happening, we would worry much less.

Arthur Roberts related to a New York City class his worry about his son, who took to the road with a knapsack on his back, as did so many youngsters in the late 1960s and early 1970s. "Doug had quit college after his freshman year. He was eighteen and was trying to find himself. After several meaningless short-term jobs, he decided to hitchhike around the United States. My wife and I were scared silly. We had read about kids being assaulted on the road. We visualized him being hit by a truck while trying to thumb a ride, falling in with drug addicts, youth gangs or other bad influences. We worried about his winding up in jail, a hospital or at worst in the morgue in some strange town far, far away. We were afraid every time the phone rang—fearing some horrible news.

"I remembered Dale Carnegie's admonition: 'Let's examine the record. Let's ask ourselves: What are the chances, according to the law of averages, that this event I am worrying about will ever occur?'

"I checked with the New York City Police Department. Their records showed that only a small fraction of the kids who took to the road ever got into any trouble. A friend who worked for the Associated Press verified that only a few of these young people made the news.

"Knowing that the law of averages was on our side, my wife and I were able to relax and accept the situation. Had we not applied this principle to our problem we would have both been complete nervous wrecks before he returned three months later."

Another frequent source of worry is fear that something will happen that might interfere with a much-anticipated pleasurable event. Brides worry incessantly that it might rain on their wedding day. Children worry that something will prevent them from going on a picnic. Parents worry that a child's illness might occur just as they plan to leave for a vacation. Of course these things do occur. It does rain on some wedding days; a picnic is cancelled because Dad had to go out of town on business; a youngster does come down with the measles at vacation time, but the chances of any of these occurring to a specific person are infinitesimal.

In a final talk to a Garden City, New York, class, Stan

Elman told of his worry that he might lose his deposit on an air trip he was planning.

The airline had offered a substantial discount if tickets were purchased several months before a trip. Cancellation would result in a financial penalty. He worried for months about all of the possibilities that would cause him to have to cancel the trip and lose the money. Of course, nothing happened and he went on the vacation. "If only I had been aware of Dale Carnegie's teachings about worry then," Elman said, "I would have realized how remote the chances were of any of the things I feared actually happening and all those days and nights of worry would have been avoided."

Failure or unwillingness to accept a situation which cannot be changed is another great cause of worry. To worry about something about which nothing can be done is not only frustrating but dangerous to one's mental and physical health. Carnegie admonishes his readers to *cooperate with the inevitable*.

Marion J. Van Wormer of Doylestown, Pennsylvania, faced her new widowhood as one might expect. Her husband had died suddenly leaving her with two small children. Not unexpectedly, she had been feeling sorry for herself. She remembered how enthusiastic her husband had been about his experience as a student and a graduate assistant with the Dale Carnegie Course. He had often quoted one of Dale Carnegie's principles on worry. *Cooperate with the inevitable*. There was no point in brooding. Mrs. Van Wormer enrolled in the Course. It helped her to overcome her fears and to face life with some confidence and less worry.

This principle can best be summarized in the priceless prayer written by Dr. Reinhold Niebuhr:

> God grant me the serenity
> To accept the things I cannot change,

> The courage to change the things I can,
> And the wisdom to know the difference.

A corollary to this principle is the old adage, *Don't try to saw sawdust.* Once a bad situation is accepted and we know it cannot be changed, there is no point fretting about it.

Erica Peters was a concert pianist. She had graduated from the famous Juilliard School of Music and was launched on a concert career. After the birth of her first child, she suffered a stroke which completely paralyzed her for several months. Her recovery was slow, but in due course she was able to resume a normal life—except that the fingers of her right hand were permanently weakened by the brain damage and she could no longer play the piano professionally.

Instead of brooding over this tremendous blow to her life's goal, she recognized she could not do anything to change it. Rather than try to saw sawdust, Erica turned her education and talents to teaching piano. Today she is a successful and very happy teacher of the piano.

Paraphrasing the old nursery rhyme: *All the king's horses and all the king's men can't put the past together again.* Write off what cannot be changed and start over again with the strengths you have.

J. Edwin ("Whit") Whitlow, who was the Carnegie sponsor in Hawaii for many years and subsequently a consultant, exemplifies the application of this philosophy. In 1974 he became very ill while on a consulting assignment in the United States. The doctors could not diagnose his ailment. Upon returning to Hawaii, he underwent exploratory surgery and had several abscesses removed which had been poisoning his system. This left him very weak and at his age (then early seventies) it seemed unlikely that he would ever make a full recovery.

"On January 7, 1975," Whitlow reported, "Nick Lisante (a member of the staff of Dale Carnegie & Associates, Inc.) visited me on his way to Japan. I was really sick. My nerves were shot. I could hardly carry on a conversation. I asked Nick when he was coming back from Japan. He said he would be in Hawaii again on January 28. I promised him that Viona (Mrs. Whitlow) and I would take him out to dinner then. Nick didn't believe me. But when he returned we did take him out for a good Hawaiian meal.

"How did I do it? The day after Nick left I said to myself: 'You can do one of two things: become a feeble old man and sit here and never get well or you can get up and do something about it. That day I got Viona to help me walk a few steps. Each day I walked a little more. Finally I was able to walk one mile a day; then two miles and I increased this day by day. One day I did fifteen miles. I've walked at least four miles each day ever since. I am now in full health, conduct my consulting business and travel all over the world. I attribute this to my determination."

Another cause of worry is the resentment people have when others are unappreciative. Jack Morano told his Carnegie class in Allentown, Pennsylvania, how he wasted five years of his life brooding over the ingratitude of his nephews. When Jack was sixty he decided to celebrate his birthday by giving presents instead of getting them. He had no children of his own, so he gave each of his three nephews $100. After expressing surprise and saying thanks the gift was never mentioned again. They didn't visit him or even telephone and on his next birthday he didn't even receive birthday cards from them. For five years he brooded about this ingratitude. It never left his thoughts. He talked about it to his friends; he dreamed about it at night. It made his whole life unpleasant.

After reading *How to Stop Worrying and Start Living,* he recognized that this was not unusual. Dale Carnegie reminds us that when Christ healed ten lepers in one afternoon, only one even stopped to thank him. If we go around expecting gratitude we are headed straight for a lot of heartaches. Carnegie suggests that if we want to find happiness, let's stop thinking about gratitude or ingratitude and give for the inner joy of giving.

Morano, like so many others who accept this, began to live a happier life when he no longer expected too much gratitude from others.

How many times have we heard the expression: *Count Your Blessings*. Too often we take our advantages and assets for granted. If we count our blessings and use our strengths we can overcome our worries.

About 90 percent of the things in our lives are right and 10 percent are wrong. If we want to be happy we have to concentrate on the 90 percent that are right and ignore the other 10 percent.

Valerie Swanson had come to New York from her home in a small community in Minnesota to start a career in the theater. In high school she had been the star in the drama group; she had been selected homecoming queen in her junior, and again in her senior year. After two years at a local community college where she had excellent grades and starred in the annual drama production, she decided to enroll in the American Academy of Dramatic Arts. Here, in competition with other highly talented young men and women, she did not fare so well. She told her Dale Carnegie classmates: "I was pretty, had moderate talent, some experience, but compared to those other kids, I just didn't have what it takes to be a real success in the theater. I worried and brooded for weeks. I couldn't sleep and this made my work at the academy even worse. Finally, a few months ago I just quit. I was afraid to tell my folks, but I realized that I couldn't keep taking the money they were sending me if I was not in school. So I started looking for a job. But what could I do? I didn't have any of the skills needed for office work, or any other occupation. All my life I had dreamed and planned for a career in the theater.

"After many frustrations, a woman at an employment agency took an interest in me. She suggested I evaluate my strengths. Her advice was: 'Remember the words of a song that was popular a few years ago—*Accentuate the positive; eliminate the negative.*'

"I looked back at my short life to determine what my positives were. I recalled all the pleasure I had in being on stage. I had the ability to talk fluently before groups. I was fairly intelligent—at least my school grades were high. Instead of worrying about my lack of real talent in the theater, I started thinking about how I could capitalize on those assets. I decided to go back to school for a teacher's certificate. To finance this I took a refresher course in typing and have now obtained a job as a receptionist. I count my blessings. I'm looking to the future when I can use these strengths toward a satisfying career."

Positive outlooks can be reinforced by doing something for other people. People who have nothing to do brood on their own troubles. Busy people, particularly those who are busy helping others, cannot dwell on their worries. A White Plains, New York, class member told her story: "Eight years ago, I was desperately unhappy," Mrs. Ruth Flohr told the class. "My children were grown up and did not need me. I felt completely unfulfilled.

"Early one Sunday morning, my neighbor called, crying and incoherent. I ran to her house and found her walking around in a daze, obviously very ill. I got her to bed and called the doctor. For the next four days I ran between our two houses taking care of her, as well as my own family. By the fourth day she was feeling better and as I gave her a back rub, she said, 'You know, you should have been a nurse.'

"From that moment on the idea of being a nurse was all I could think of. The following week, I went to a nearby hospital and offered to do volunteer work there. I loved it! At the end of the year I applied and was accepted in their school of practical nursing. It was the hardest year of my life. I had to be at the hospital by 7 A.M. When I got home at four, there were household chores to be done. In addition, I had three or four hours of homework each night. Many times during that year I wanted to quit. Another woman and I were the two oldest in the class and we frequently had to give each other pep talks to keep going. We both made it! Graduation day was one of the happiest in my life. My family and friends were all there.

"Since then I've gone on to become a registered nurse and obtain my associate's degree in nursing, and now I am working and studying for my bachelor's degree in nursing. My family troubles and my feelings about lack of fulfillment disappeared with my involvement in my new career."

Often people are faced with situations over which they have no control and which bring much sorrow into their lives. Dale Carnegie did not offer Pollyanna-like solutions to such situations. He knew that suffering is part of life and one cannot eliminate it. His advice was to learn to cope with problems and accept the inevitable: not to brood and worry over them, as to do so would do more harm than the problem itself.

Celima Singleton of Beaumont, Texas, hit a low point in her life when she learned that her son, John, was deaf. "I could not accept the fact that he was deaf," she commented. "I became depressed, cried a lot and could think of nothing else. Day and night all that went through my mind was that my baby was deaf. He would never hear music, never hear the birds sing, never even hear my voice.

"As a result I developed an ulcer. My doctor knew his psychology. He said: 'O.K., John is deaf. What can you do about it? The answer is nothing because John has nerve deafness for which there is no cure. You can worry yourself into a nervous breakdown, but if you do you will not be able to help John and he needs your help now.' I knew I had to take more definite action to snap out of my depression.

"I volunteered to work at a center for handicapped children. There I saw children who were blind as well as deaf, children who were crippled and confined to wheelchairs, deformed children and children with brain damage. I realized that my John was not as badly off as many of these children. It dawned on me that I had much to be thankful for. When you get to feeling sorry for yourself, just look around the corner, there's always somebody that has a problem worse than yours.

Dale Carnegie reinforces this admonition by suggesting we compare what appear to be problems to us with those of people whose problems are much worse than ours. He quotes an anonymous poem:

> I had the blues because I had no shoes
> Until upon the street, I met a man who had no feet.

A common reason why people worry is that they try to emulate and be somebody else. Each one of us must be himself or herself. We cannot be exactly like another person. Trying to do something in a manner which is unnatural to us cannot succeed.

Emerson summed this up in his essay "Self-Reliance:" "There is a time in every man's education when he arrives at the conviction that envy is ignorance; that imitation is suicide; that he must take himself for better or for worse, as his portion; that though the wide universe is full of good, no kernal of nourishing corn can come to him but through his toil bestowed upon that plot of ground which is given him to till. The power which resides in him is new in nature and none but he knows what that is which he can do, nor does he know until he has tried."

One of the most quoted of Dale Carnegie's principles is: *If you have a lemon, make a lemonade.* All of us are handed lemons from time to time. The fool takes it and says, "I'm beaten. It's fate. I haven't got a chance." Then he storms against the world, berating his bad luck and indulging in an orgy of self-pity. But the wise person, when handed a lemon asks, "What lesson can I learn from this misfortune? How can I improve my situation? How can I turn this lemon into a lemonade?"

Dale Carnegie tells the story of Thelma Thompson who accompanied her husband when he was stationed at an army base near the Mojave Desert. "My husband was ordered out on maneuvers in the desert and I was left alone in a tiny shack. The heat was unbearable—125 degrees in the shade of a cactus. Not a soul to talk to except Mexicans and Indians and they couldn't speak English. I was so utterly wretched that I wrote to my parents that I was giving up and coming home. My father answered my letter with just two lines—two lines that will always sing in my memory—two lines that completely altered my life:

> Two men looked out from prison bars
> One saw the mud, the other saw the stars.

"I read those lines over and over. I was ashamed of myself. I made up my mind I would find out what was good in my present situation; I would look for the stars.

"I made friends with the natives and their reaction amazed me. When I showed interest in their weaving and pottery, they gave me presents of their favorite pieces which they had refused to sell to tourists. I studied the fascinating forms of the cactus and the yuccas and the Joshua trees. I learned about prairie dogs, watched for the desert sunsets, and hunted for seashells that had been left there millions of years ago when the sands of the desert had been an ocean floor.

"What brought about the astonishing change in me? The Mojave Desert hadn't changed. The Indians hadn't changed. But I had. I had changed my attitude of mind. And by doing so, I transformed a wretched experience into the most exciting adventure of my life. I was stimulated and excited by this new world that I had discovered. I was so excited I wrote a book about it—a novel that was published under the title *Bright Ramparts.* I had looked out of my self-created prison and found the stars."[2]

Turning lemons into lemonade isn't always easy. It may not always succeed, but we ought to try anyway. We have everything to gain and nothing to lose.

Reason One: We may succeed—and we often do.

Reason Two: Even if we don't succeed, the mere attempt to turn a minus into a plus will cause us to look forward instead of backward; it will replace negative thoughts with positive thoughts; it will release creative energy and spur us to get so busy that we won't have either the time or the inclination to mourn over what is past and forever gone.

In *How to Stop Worrying and Start Living,* Carnegie also tackles the problem of fatigue and boredom as a cause of worry. Dale Carnegie not only preached avoiding fatigue by frequent rests, but he practiced it in his daily life.

Murray Mosser tells of one of his early encounters with Mr. Carnegie. "After our meeting in the afternoon, Mr. Carnegie accompanied me to my room at the hotel. He told me he would like to rest before the evening meeting. He took off his coat, loosened his tie, opened his collar, took out from his pocket a black silk cloth and covered his eyes with it. Within minutes he was asleep."

Dale Carnegie believed that taking frequent rests would

[2] Dale Carnegie, *How to Stop Worrying and Start Living* (New York: Simon and Schuster, 1944), pp. 128–29.

prevent fatigue. In his manual, *How to Teach the Dale Carnegie Course*, he suggests that instructors rest before each class so they will have the vigor necessary for the long session. "If you can't go home for a rest, then, if possible, go to a Turkish bath or an athletic club for a massage, a rest and a nap. Before teaching a class, rest is far more important than food.

"If necessary, stretch out and rest on the floor or on three or four straight chairs placed together, or on top of an office desk."

Carnegie suggests four good working habits that will prevent fatigue and worry:

(1) Clear your desk of all papers except those relating to the immediate problem at hand.
(2) Do things in order of their importance.
(3) When you face a problem, solve it then and there if you have the facts necessary to make a decision. Don't keep putting off decisions.
(4) Learn to organize, deputize and supervise.

These principles are expanded in the Dale Carnegie Management Seminar.

When a person enrolls in the Dale Carnegie Course, he or she completes a form in which they indicate why they are taking the course and what they intend to get out of it. Surprisingly, only a few write that their objective is to overcome worry. Yet, at the final session when they report on what they found most helpful in the course a good number of students say that the book and talks on overcoming worry were significant in their lives.

People sometimes worry about things that really do not matter. They stress some facets of their life out of proportion and constantly fret about it. Sandra Murphy, who took the Dale Carnegie Course in New Jersey, relates her obsession with her "large nose."

"I used to tape it up, thinking perhaps it would grow up,

but it didn't. I wouldn't let people look at me from the side. All through school I was concerned about my nose.

"After school I entered the business world—still concerned about my nose. If only I had a pretty nose, people would like and love me. Finally I decided to have plastic surgery done on it. At the hospital, they broke my nose, put a file up my nose and filed away at the cartilege. Afterwards I had black eyes and swollen cheeks for several weeks.

"Six months later I had a second operation on my nose since the first didn't come out quite right. Six months after that I had an auto accident, broke my nose and had to have a third operation.

"Three operations on my nose with the hope that I would be pretty! And would you believe it, when I went home my mother and my friends didn't even notice a change!

"Those people who like me still like me. Those who had not noticed me before still pay little attention to me. The lesson I learned was that people like you for what you are, not what you look like and it was unfortunate I wasted so many years brooding about my nose."

Psychologists, clergymen and other counselors have often advised persons with problems to talk about them. The idea behind this is that the catharsis of talking can help them to see their problems in perspective. This was demonstrated in a talk given by Kim Brandt, who took the Dale Carnegie Course in Falls Church, Virginia. She told of the breakup of her five-year engagement to the man she had planned to marry. She had loved him very much and was deeply hurt by his desertion.

"It was about that time that I started reading *How to Stop Worrying and Start Living.* It saved my life. I tried everything from not dwelling on the past, to living one day at a time, to keeping busy. They all helped me very much, but my advice to you would be to try all of them, but most of all to share it with a friend as I have shared this with you. It may be painful, but the sense of relief is well worth it."

Bill Alvarez of Albuquerque, New Mexico, was a constant worrier. He had developed quite a case of ulcers. Once exposed to the Dale Carnegie principles he applied them in his daily life. *Don't fuss with trifles, Live in day-tight compartments, Cooperate with the inevitable* became part of his approach to his work and life. By the time the course was completed his ulcers had disappeared. When he went back to his doctor, the physician couldn't believe it. "Bill," he said, "this is a miracle. You cured your ulcers." Bill answered "Yes, I've got me a new doctor." His physician said, "Oh, really. What's his name?" And Bill replied, "Dr. Dale Carnegie."

9

Carnegie Training— Why It Works

If we think happy thoughts, we will be happy. If we think miserable thoughts, we will be miserable. If we think fear thoughts, we will be fearful. If we think failure, we will certainly fail. If we wallow in self-pity, everyone will want to shun us and avoid us.   —DALE CARNEGIE

When a program has been as successful as the Dale Carnegie courses have been, there must be a philosophy of education that has made it work. It couldn't possibly be a matter of chance.

Dale Carnegie was a pioneer in adult education. Having studied to be a teacher in his youth, he became familiar with the educational philosophers of his day. Over the years, he experimented with new approaches and adopted those that were in line with his own objectives.

From the start, he was interested in John Dewey's "learn by doing" philosophy. He recognized that adults learn best through personal involvement in the learning process. Dale Carnegie did not believe in the traditional lecture approach to teaching. Instructors in Carnegie programs are cautioned against lecturing. They are taught that a lecture only superimposes the instructor's knowledge on the class but does not assure that it is being learned. All class members must be encouraged to participate in order to derive the maximum benefits of the training. This participation ranges from personal reports, to group exercises, to role playing, and in some courses, to table discussions.

Individual differences are recognized and class members are taught to check themselves at any point with the way they felt before the training—not with other members of the group. This prevents feelings of inferiority that may be caused by comparison with others who appear to be making better progress. The instructor helps class members by showing them how much they have improved in each session. Class members' goals are defined in the early sessions; the instructor keeps these in mind and points out how each succeeding session contributes to the attainment of the desired goals.

Instructors motivate class members to want to achieve their goals by stressing the benefits, and showing how particular learning situations develop skills, or change attitudes that produce results. After each talk, the instructor makes specific mention of the progress made. A student may have indicated a desire to deal more effectively with those working under him in his job as the reason for taking the Course. After a talk in which the student describes the application of a principle of better human relations, the instructor will comment as follows: "Didn't Joe show real sensitivity toward the feelings of his co-workers in that incident?" This endorses Joe's leadership methods and earns the approval of the entire class.

Instructors in Carnegie courses are positive, encouraging, approving and optimistic. They strive to improve each class member's capability on the spot, while the situation described is before them. After each talk a very brief comment from the instructor—often just one or two sentences—points out to the speaker and the class the key accomplishment in the situation described. The comment is made right after the talk because psychological studies have proven that comments made immediately will elicit a much higher rate of acceptance and retention than those made at a later time. This is the heart of Dale Carnegie instruction, for it is at this point that the learning process becomes alive and the participant is made aware of his or her own responses and capabilities.

If learning only occurred and stopped in the classroom, the Carnegie program would be just like any other in education. But it is not like any other program because what the participants learn is carried over into every other aspect of their lives. It is the instructor's responsibility to ensure that class members make sincere, meaningful and practical application in their own lives of what they have learned. The course is structured in learning series, from the simple to the complex, and the application comes before, during and after a session. For instance: a human relations principle is discussed at one session, studied in the literature between sessions, put into practice before the next session, reported on during a session and, as a result of the group dynamics that is generated, practical application is almost automatic.

Dr. L. Gray Burdin, former vice president of Dale Carnegie & Associates, Inc., in charge of instruction (now retired), explained the educational philosophy behind the Dale Carnegie courses as based on several major psychological philosophies:

It is a pragmatic program following the teachings of C. S. Pierce and William James. Instead of delving into the psychological reasons for the process followed, the student is given an easily understood principle to follow. As an example: A student is told to select a subject he knows and is eager to talk about. The philosophical background of this principle is that people will be more at ease and feel self-confident talking about something with which they are familiar, rather than one about which they know little. However, the student is only aware that this is a pragmatic way to select a subject.

In establishing each course, Dale Carnegie aimed to give participants the skills he believed they needed to help them achieve their goals. The instructor is thoroughly trained in the use of the methods, techniques and tools to help the class members attain their goals. One thing is certain: The Course is not mechanistic or rigid. Carnegie's insistence on inner growth as a prelude to action protects the individuality of each class member.

Dorothy Carnegie expressed this philosophy; "We can't change personality—and we wouldn't if we could. All we can do is to help a person use more effectively whatever abilities and natural assets he or she has. By throwing off the constrictions of fear, a person is able to express whatever he or she wants to express; and by this means the total personality is engaged for total self-fulfillment. The joy and power of this new freedom of self-expression often changes a person's way of living, thinking and acting: the person himself is not 'changed'—but just uses his or her own resources to a greater extent than ever before. We cannot give people qualities they do not possess within themselves, but we can make them aware of their own qualities and inspire them to use them."

Dale Carnegie training is based on self-assuredness, on an acceptance of oneself as a person of worth, who can achieve desired goals through greater understanding of oneself. This is accomplished pragmatically in the classroom. Students get to know the principles for motivating others, and as they develop their own motivating skills in expressing ideas forcefully, they feel more sure of themselves and become happier and more productive members of society. Life becomes a challenge, a job ceases to be routine, and family relationships acquire warmth and meaning.

The Carnegie method also borrows from the Gestalt school. The gestaltists or "configurationists" believe that the total configuration of a situation should be considered, rather than in its separate components. "The whole," they quote, "is greater than the sum of its parts."

This concept is implemented in the Dale Carnegie courses through the instructors, who are concerned with the *total individual* While most courses in speech or public speaking devote considerable time to such matters as eye contact with the audience, foot position, use of notes, and the like, Carnegie talks are chiefly concerned with overcoming fear, conveying sincerity, expressing enthusiasm, and with a broad series of general reactions while speaking. Hence the Dale Carnegie Course is not primarily a course in public speaking but one of self-development. The talk is really a vehicle to help the class members express themselves and master a situation. If emphasis is placed on particular parts of a talk instead of the talk as a whole (or on the person who gives the talk) the class may remember just some comments on what is trivial, and learn very little about what is real and important in a situation. By recognizing and concentrating on the "gestalt" (the whole situation) instead of its components, the instructor brings out a positive reaction from the students.

Another important philosophical foundation of the Carnegie teaching method is autosuggestion. This was an idea promulgated by Emile Coué early in the twentieth century. Coué's idea was that one's "inward conversation" determined how one felt about oneself and formed the basis of an action or actions.

In other words, if a person thinks "I'm a failure," a failure will result. If a person thinks "I'm no good," that person will be no good. If one thinks "I'm a has-been," one will act as a has-been.

On the other hand, if one thinks "I can succeed, I am improving and getting better and better," then one will certainly succeed. Coué's most famous suggestion for "inward conversation" was: "Every day in every way I am getting better and better," repeated over and over again.

The Dale Carnegie Course offers several ways of using this idea. From the beginning each class member is encouraged by the instructor's comments and the applause of the classmates. All are given the courage to overcome their difficulties. No one is permitted to return to his or her seat without feeling that something worthwhile has been accomplished. This spirit is reinforced by the other speakers. When a speaker sees that others are successful, confidence in success is built up. The optimism and enthusiasm generated in the class reach each member and therefore the class as a whole. This "internal" or "auto" suggestion makes for unqualified success.

Another method is even more direct. In the session on enthusiasm students are taught to give themselves pep talks before getting up to talk before the class. Many students report that they give themselves pep talks before undertaking an important activity. Salespeople give themselves pep talks before visiting a prospect; an employee gives himself or herself a pep talk before asking for a raise; a job applicant reported that the pep talk she gave herself before her interview helped her to land a job.

Because a person must feel successful to be successful, Dale Carnegie instructors strive to make each class member feel a sense of achievement after each talk. Their comments concentrate on the positive factors. No attention is paid to gestures per se, to breathing, posture, outlines, notes, stance or type of speech. All comments are geared to the strong points of the talk as a whole. With this attitude, a feeling of confidence is easily built up. Students look forward to each class; they carry within them the confidence they have built up from session to session until, by the end of the Course (or even before the end), this confidence becomes part of their total life pattern.

Dale Carnegie used this confidence-building method long before B. F. Skinner's theory of operant conditioning was promulgated. Good points are rewarded and reinforced immediately. Bad points are ignored, and in time the student establishes the good points as habits. Awards are given in each class to the class members who show the most improvement. In addition, there are special awards for achievement in human relations and for controlling worry. These awards are highly treasured by winners, as evidence of confidence in themselves. The atmosphere of approval and approbation also engenders positive attitudes.

In each session of the Dale Carnegie Course, every member participates two and occasionally three times by talking before a group, either impromptu or with preparation. There are no lectures in the Course. The instructors are limited to very brief—approximately one-minute—introductory remarks or comments after each talk. Results are noted only through the participation of class members at every session.

Three textbooks are used to supplement class activity. These are: *The Quick and Easy Way to Effective Speaking, How to Win Friends and Influence People* and *How to Stop Worrying and Start Living.* In addition, booklets on special subjects are distributed in preparation for specific sessions. The most important of these booklets is the *Course Guide* which outlines each session and gives the students their assignments.

The speaking assignments are based on the actual experience of class members, by means of which they gain insights into their own development and motivation. From a listener's point of view the other class members recognize the similarity of their experience to those that are being talked about. They don't consider themselves unique because of fear in certain situations. Class members also note the value of applying the rules and principles taught, since the speakers themselves give concrete evidence of their workability and the benefits derived from them in their personal and working lives.

All of this group interaction is carried out in an atmosphere of approval generated in the main by the instructor.

Criticism, in its negative sense, is not used. Strengths are emphasized and correction, when it is needed, is indirect, and accomplished without abrasiveness. In this atmosphere of acceptance, individuals are encouraged to express themselves freely and to be themselves.

The first third of the Course is devoted to building up the confidence of the class members. They are asked to undertake increasingly challenging assignments that are designed to build confidence and conquer fear. One of the most difficult tasks in speaking before a group is the need to build confidence. Since speaking is one of the most universal means of dealing and communicating with individuals, it is easy to see how courage is necessary for daily living.

When confidence has been established, the emphasis changes to the present and future, with considerable concentration in the Course on the use of human relations, on principles for avoiding worry, on memory for names, on the-factor of enthusiasm, and on more positive thinking in all one's dealings with others. The speaking assignments, which in earlier sessions were based on one's early life, now center around activities between sessions and on job and home situations.

During each session the instructor acts as a catalyst, stirring the class into action and response to the talks. The instructor uses two tools in making people believe in themselves and their abilities. One is by means of comments, and the other is by direct and immediate assistance.

In a recent Dale Carnegie Course session in New York City, the instructor demonstrated the effectiveness of commenting. A student, Mary H., had just completed a talk. Although her subject matter was interesting, Mary had been stiff and without animation while giving her talk. She used her hands awkwardly. The instructor commented after the talk as follows: "Class, did you see the kind of progress Mary showed? She used her hands. This shows she wanted to get across to us that she was experiencing the incident she spoke of. She relived her experience, even to acting it out. Now watch her repeat her success. She may even exaggerate to make her story clearer. It's easy for her now. Here's how she'll do it." (At this point the instructor gave a ten-second demonstration). "All right, Mary. You're the teacher. Show us!"

Mary repeated part of her talk with much greater animation and the use of gestures. After the class, the instructor discussed this with his graduate assistants. "Had I said to Mary, 'You made a fine talk, but you could do better by becoming more animated,' she would have felt she had failed and become resistant. More important she would have felt that she was weak. By telling her and the class that she was good but could do even better, she didn't even consider it criticism. She was carried away in a wave of success. Her attitude was positive and she let herself go without knowing it. Also, her classmates did not consider this drill negative for Mary. It was an affirmation not a denigration. Other members of the class accept similar drills and comments without feeling that they have been criticized or made to feel inferior."

Instructors often supplement comments with quotations from famous writers, including, of course, Dale Carnegie. These quotations give credibility to their comments, thereby demonstrating to students that these quotations reveal fundamental truths. This is particularly true in areas of human relations where the speaker, in applying one of the principles learned from Dale Carnegie's writings, is anxious to have the approval of the listeners.

Who are the people who teach the Dale Carnegie Course? They come chiefly from executive and managerial ranks. Some come from the professions and others from the sales field, from banks, education and government. They are, of course, graduates of the Course, who have been chosen for their special qualifications to undergo the rigid training required of all instructors. This training program lasts about two years, and is continued at intervals as long as they teach.

One of the primary requirements is a university degree. Many of the instructors have graduate degrees. After graduating from the Course, the potential instructor must act as a graduate assistant for at least two full courses. The graduate assistant assists the instructor by giving demonstration talks, counseling students on their talks, timing the talks and performing other duties in the classroom. They must participate in an Instructor Training Conference which is conducted by a member of the staff of the Department of Instruction at the International Headquarters. This conference is highly demanding and many candidates are eliminated if they cannot meet the high standards set by the trainer. Those who are accepted are certified as probationary instructors and may teach one or two classes in tandem with a regular instructor. Satisfactory performance as a probationary instructor earns permission to teach as a regular instructor.

Even regular instructors are subject to continuing training. Evaluations and refreshers are conducted periodically. Instructor trainers not only reinforce their basic training, but evaluate themselves and make specific suggestions to improve their instructional methods. In addition to these training refreshers, representatives of the Department of Instruction make periodic visits to sponsors throughout the world and work with instructors. Instructors are constantly being reviewed and evaluated, and may be dropped if they do not meet the standards.

Most of the Dale Carnegie sponsorships and the Department of Instruction of Dale Carnegie & Associates, Inc., are accredited by the Council for Noncollegiate Continuing Education, an accrediting body approved by the U.S. Office of Education. This organization was incorporated in 1974 as a national nonprofit organization to promote and maintain high quality in continuing education programs. To do this, they have set standards which organizations engaged in adult education must meet.

These standards are similar to those that universities and colleges must meet for accreditation. They include study of curricula, selection and training of instructors, facilities for teaching, financial stability, and results of training. To qualify, an organization must provide detailed analysis of its activities and accept visits by a team of professionals who evaluate the program as it is conducted.

The instruction standards and the educational philosophy of the Dale Carnegie Course can best be validated by the graduation rate of those who start and continue the Course. Where most adult education courses graduate only about 50 to 60 percent, the average graduation rate for the Dale Carnegie Course is 86 percent. The majority of the classes graduate 95 to 100 percent.

10

Carnegie
Around the World

The world is filled with such interesting things to do. Don't lead a dull life in such a thrilling world. —DALE CARNEGIE

The influence of Dale Carnegie's teachings is worldwide. His book, *How to Win Friends and Influence People,* has been published in thirty-six languages as well as in English; and his *How to Stop Worrying and Start Living* has been translated into twenty-seven languages. The Dale Carnegie courses are now offered in fifty countries on all five continents.

This worldwide international teaching program marks an unparalleled development in modern adult education. Throughout all the varied languages and translations, the Dale Carnegie courses remain unchanged in their essential meanings. Whether given in the staid atmosphere of a British meeting hall or in a thatch-roofed hut in a primitive village, whether taught in the heat of the tropics or the wintry climate of Scandinavia, the basics of the courses are the same.

In one way or another, through its classes and the individuals who conduct them, Dale Carnegie courses have influenced the peoples of the world in many enriching and important ways that affect the betterment of mankind.

As the courses are offered in remote parts of the world, people who had no idea who Dale Carnegie was or what his program was have discovered a new approach to adult education that results in improving the lifestyle, the status and the self-awareness of countless individuals.

Many high government officials in countries throughout the world have taken Dale Carnegie training. Cabinet members, Supreme Court justices, members of parliament and high ranking diplomats are numbered among the graduates. Both the president of Honduras, General Policarpo Paz Garcia, and his predecessor, Juan Alberto Melgar Castro, are graduates of the Dale Carnegie Course. President Paz's wife, Carlotta, is also a Dale Carnegie graduate.

Dale Carnegie courses have been held in the midst of wars, rebellions, floods and earthquakes. In July 1958 the Carnegie organization gave its first class in Havana with Drex Gibson as the instructor. Unfortunately, Fidel Castro opened with a bigger flourish six months later. Despite the turmoil resulting from the revolution, classes were held until October 1960. Toward the end of that period it was necessary to hold the classes in secret. A few months later Gibson was arrested by the police and spent five months of horror in La Cabana prison, never knowing from one day to the next whether he would be "taken to the wall" to be shot. He was later released and returned to the United States.

In 1976 Guatemala suffered one of the most severe earthquakes in world history. Over twenty-three thousand people were killed and the capital, Ciudad de Guatemala, was virtually destroyed. The people of the city started to rebuild immediately; business and schools soon reopened and the Dale Carnegie sponsor in Guatemala, Carlos E. Guzman, resumed teaching.

Several weeks later while a class was in session, a slight tremor shook the city. With the horror of the recent disaster still fresh in the minds of the people, there was immediate fear that another major earthquake was about to occur. Even though the tremor lasted only a few seconds and did not recur, the class member who was speaking at the time began to panic. She became numb with fear and could not continue her talk. Señor Guzman calmly asked her a question about her talk and encouraged her by expressing interest in what she was saying. She completed her talk and sat down.

Later she reported that she had never been more frightened in her life and only because of the calm encouragement of Señor Guzman was she able to stand there in front of the class and complete the talk. She commented that this experience gave her much self-confidence. "If I could continue talking to the class under that pressure, there is nothing that can faze me in the future."

The Course was introduced in Britain in 1956 with a demonstration session at Cowdrey Hall in London. It was met with caustic comment from the British press which thought it "childish." However, as students registered, went through the course and graduated, attitudes changed, and over the ensuing years thousands of people have graduated from the courses in England.

Some of the early experiences in giving the course in non-English speaking countries were made in Central and South America. Instructors from the United States went to these countries and set up classes to be conducted in English. Naturally, only people who were fluent in English could take the courses. There were enough Americans, Englishmen and others who did speak English to warrant holding classes.

Spanish language courses were introduced as soon as bilingual instructors could be trained. All the books and materials are now available in Spanish. In the early days, however, the instructors used English materials, and even though the classes were conducted in Spanish, the conferences in which the instructors were trained, were conducted in English.

Even where students have a reasonably good command of English, it is difficult for them to express the nuances of their feelings in a strange language. The Carnegie people have encouraged teaching the courses in the language of the country. Such is the case in most major European languages as well as in Cantonese, Afrikaans, Tagalog, Icelandic, Hebrew, Indonesian, Japanese, Malayan, Swahili and Thai.

Occasionally students from other countries have doubts about whether courses so "American" as the Dale Carnegie courses are applicable to the customs and traditions of their countries.

Eduardo Criado Aguirre, sponsor of the Dale Carnegie courses in Spain, commented on this: "An unusual point about the Dale Carnegie courses is that often a participant will enroll in the program quite concerned about its being too 'North American.' This feeling, however, disappears as the Course proceeds. By the time the training is completed, each participant has identified with the course and reflects on it from his or her own viewpoint and can make the application to daily life."

In addition to sponsoring the courses in many cities in Spain, Criado writes a two-page feature article for a weekly magazine entitled "El Poder de la Personalidad" ("The Power of the Personality") which brings many of the principles of Carnegie to readers throughout Spain.

In South Africa classes are given in Afrikaans and English. Terry Ostrowiak, sponsor in Johannesburg, finds that students in South Africa sometimes use the Course to improve their English. Although this is not a purpose of the course, it gives the student greater confidence in using the English language.

From time to time Ostrowiak conducts classes in native residential areas. The sessions are conducted in English. In one class a student was giving a talk about his experience with a witch doctor. Suddenly, he called out a phrase in Zulu. The entire group rose and responded in the old tribal manner, then quietly resumed their seats, and the class was continued in English, as usual.

Today, most of the sponsors are citizens of the country in which they conduct classes, although there are still a few sponsorships held by Americans or other nationalities in foreign areas.

One of the leading sponsors in Europe is Dieter Alten whose territory covers all of West Germany. Alten was brought up in the prewar years and was taught to hate Americans. At age seventeen he enlisted in the German army, but the war ended before he had completed his basic training. He was a prisoner of war of the Americans for a short time. His exposure to Americans was limited and he had a poor attitude toward them.

In recent years as Alten has become more knowledgeable about America and Americans, he has recognized the prejudice against the "conquerors" as the cause of his feelings. Alten told a Dale Carnegie International Convention in 1973: "The Dale Carnegie Course helps people see other people as individuals not just as members of a group against which one might be prejudiced. In Carnegie one gets to meet all kinds of people from different environments and cultures—all in the same class—and one gets a different perspective."

Alten also commented on the problem of identifying with the American examples given in the books and other materials. In the translations some illustrations had to be changed to make them meaningful to German-speaking people.

It is difficult for Germans to accept the American custom of using first names with strangers. As it is the Dale Carnegie practice all over the world to use first names, Alten explains the reason in the first session. He tells his classes that the use of the first names breaks down barriers to communication in the class—but suggests that one would not use first names if one were to meet a class member on the street even though in the class he is addressed by his first name. To overcome the resistance to this informality in the class, the Germans use the formal form of address "Sie" rather than the familiar "du" when addressing class members. He also explains that the traditional greeting given by the instructor, "Good evening friends" is not an imposition on their concept of friendship (which is again more restricted in German culture), but that in the milieu of a Carnegie classroom all participants are in the true sense friends, as they are sharing a common experience in an atmosphere of friendship.

The Dale Carnegie courses have been well received in Germany. One company in Hamburg was so enthusiastic about the results it obtained from the courses that the managing director encouraged his own sales staff to recommend the training to their customers, and even gave them bonuses for each person that they enrolled in the courses.

Initial resistance to some of the Carnegie techniques is not unusual in cultures which differ markedly from the American. In England, Paul Werner, sponsor in Birmingham, reported that a fellow walked out of the class early in the "break out of your shell" session in which class members shout and pound the table. "He was a city broker, a chap who belonged to all the right clubs, very British—old school, the kind that wears a dinner jacket in the desert. I saw him walk out so I walked out with him. He said, 'If I have to do that I'm dropping out. This goes against the grain.' I responded: 'You know why we are doing this. Do you agree the purpose is good?' He nodded. 'Do you feel you ought to lose some of your false inhibitions?' He thought for a few moments and then agreed to go back. When his turn came to talk, he spoke about his resentment at having to make a talk under these circumstances. He did it well and, in turn, became one of our best boosters."

Presenting the courses in the Orient created problems different from those in the western world. The Dale Carnegie manager in Hong Kong described how difficult it was to use the traditional sales methods in dealing with the Chinese. Because they are very sensitive about "saving face," the Chinese prospect does not say "no" when they are not interested in buying because they feel that to do so would make the salesperson lose face. Instead, they equivocate and stall until the salesperson gives up.

The manager said: "This made selling a most frustrating experience. You never knew whether or not you closed the sale. We overcame this when it became apparent that the Chinese are very honest people. At our preview meetings we indicated that those persons who were interested in taking the course would receive the books used in the course after the meeting. Those who really were going to sign up took the books, the others refused the books, thus 'saving the face' of the salesperson by not having to say 'no.' "

Japan, however, is quite different. The courses are mostly attended by employees sent by their companies. In Japan, companies are very paternalistic and take a strong interest in the development of their employees. The Dale Carnegie courses have been a significant part of their business. Most of the major companies in Japan enroll employees from all levels. They sign annual contracts with the sponsor to assure that their people will be accommodated.

Classes are fully booked months in advance. To accommodate interested persons who do not work for the major companies, a small percentage of each class is open to the public. However, applicants for these few vacancies are carefully screened by the sponsor, Yukinaga ("Frank") Mochizuki.

Mr. Mochizuki first came across the Dale Carnegie Course when he was a student at Michigan State University's School of Hotel Management. He took the course in Chicago and it left such a strong impression on him that he felt it should be given in Japan. Some years later he wrote to the Dale Carnegie International Headquarters suggesting that they offer it in his country. The letter was turned over to J. Edwin Whitlow, then sponsor in Hawaii and the nearest Carnegie representative to Japan. Whitlow corresponded with and later visited Mr. Mochizuki in Tokyo. They discussed the possibility of his joining Whitlow's organization and selling and teaching the Course in Japan. As he was functioning as a hotel management consultant and was very successful, he was reluctant to give this up and start a new business. He also did not feel he was ready to undertake this venture at that time. Eight months later, after serious deliberation, he made the decision to go ahead with this project.

Frank Mochizuki has twelve instructors on his staff, all are bilingual in English and Japanese and all but one are Japanese. The non-Japanese instructor is an official in the United States embassy and is, of course, fluent in Japanese. When President Ford and Secretary of State Kissinger visited Japan in 1975, this official arranged for the entire Dale Carnegie staff to attend the reception at the embassy.

Although in most of the countries where Dale Carnegie courses are given, instructors speak reasonably good English, in some areas instructor training has to be given in the native tongue. As most of the instructor trainers are not fluent in languages other than English, simultaneous translation is required. Nick Lisante, an instructor trainer who has travelled around the world several times training Carnegie staff members, tells of the strange feeling of communicating complex concepts through translators. "In Paris, our sponsor, Gerard Weyne, and his associate, Gilbert Jourdan, acted as simultaneous interpreters. At first it was distracting to have to wait for the translations and not to be able to make direct response to inquiries. However, once I became accustomed to this, it went surprisingly well and was a most productive meeting."

In some countries students come from far distances to attend classes. In Australia it is not unusual for class members to fly their own planes from distant sheep stations to Melbourne or to another major city. In some small communities where there were not enough people to warrant holding classes, groups of interested students would charter a bus to come to the nearest town where a class was being held.

Financing the course has been a problem in some countries. The income levels of the great mass of the population in some areas are too low for them to afford the cost of the course. To help overcome this, sponsors work hard to get companies to pay part or all of the tuition for their employees. In England, Stanley Ibbotson, sponsor for Leeds, reports that the government encourages training by establishing boards to help finance adult education. The government rebates 50 percent of the cost of a course to students who successfully complete it.

Another country in which the Dale Carnegie courses have been very well received is Iceland. The sponsor for Iceland, Konrad Adolphsson, celebrated his tenth anniversary with Carnegie on January 9, 1976, with a formal dinner dance to which he had invited almost three hundred graduates of his classes. The principal speaker was a member of the Icelandic cabinet who commented on how much the Dale Carnegie courses had meant to Iceland. A large number of government and business leaders in Iceland are graduates, including a former president and many members of the cabinet.

Ninety-five percent of Adolphsson's business comes from enthusiastic graduates. He seldom, if ever, makes a sales call. Konrad Adolphsson has a group of Dale Carnegie graduates which he affectionately calls his "army." These are people who form temporary and informal clubs of Dale Carnegie graduates. It is not like an alumni association in any sense because people move in and out of these clubs as they go on to other opportunities. So, generally, the clubs are peopled by recent Carnegie graduates. There are currently about thirteen such clubs operating in Iceland.

Richard D. Morgal, vice president of Dale Carnegie & Associates, Inc., flew to Iceland for the anniversary party and addressed the meeting in Icelandic expressing the good wishes of Carnegie people all over the world to Adolphsson and his people.

A few months later, a similar party was held by Tony Stemp, the sponsor in Durban, South Africa, to celebrate his twenty-first year with Dale Carnegie. South Africa has been a highly active area for Dale Carnegie courses and there are sponsors or area managers in every major city in this country.

Because of government policies and local customs, separate classes were held for whites, blacks and other races for many years. In 1976 Tony Stemp enrolled sixty Indians and thirty whites in two classes which were to start at the same time. As none of the class members—white or Indian—objected, Stemp divided the group into equal numbers and the first two integrated classes were held in Durban.

Subsequently, white, black, colored (persons with mixed racial backgrounds) and Asians have been enrolled in the same classes in Durban and in other South African cities. Stemp reports that as this often is the very first time persons of one race had any real contact with those of other races, it has fostered a much better understanding of cultural similarities and differences among class members.

One of the largest groups ever to graduate from Dale Carnegie courses at one ceremony were awarded diplomas in Guayaquil, Ecuador, in 1975. Nine classes, consisting of approximately 380 people, participated in the event, which was extremely well organized. More than one thousand people including families and friends of the graduates attended the special function, which was held at the Navy Club of

Guayaquil. Many Ecuadorian dignitaries were present, including a justice of the Supreme Court of Ecuador and the country's chief assessor.

When all the diplomas had been awarded to each of the classes, there were class yells and songs, followed by a snake dance like those often performed at football games. Special presentations were made to the sponsor, Ricardo Piño, and his associate, Eduardo Mendoza.

John Cooper, then executive vice president of Dale Carnegie & Associates, Inc., and his wife, Edna, were invited to attend the graduation. They were greeted at the airport by a crowd of approximately eight hundred Carnegie graduates, their families and friends. After being shepherded through the airport, they found themselves surrounded by another welcoming crowd. This one, waving flags, formed a motorcade and with horns blowing escorted the group to the hotel where festivities continued in the hotel lobby with the crowd dancing to the music of a band hired for the occasion.

Israel is another country in which the Dale Carnegie courses have been received enthusiastically. Dalia Ailon (now Mrs. Isack Levy) is a native-born Israeli who came to the United States with her parents when she was sixteen. After Dalia was graduated from Columbia University her parents (both Carnegie graduates) gave her as a graduation gift an enrollment in the Dale Carnegie Course. She was so enthralled by the Course that she felt it should be offered in Israel.

Over the next few years she tried to interest several people in this project. Dale Carnegie licenses, however, are not for sale. Sponsors in the United States and in most other countries have to work their way up through the ranks over many years to qualify. Occasionally, an overseas sponsor might be appointed without the long apprenticeship, but even in these rare cases a long training period is essential before they can offer and teach the courses. Miss Ailon found that none of the people she approached were willing to undertake this extensive training. They were already established in businesses and could not devote the necessary time to Carnegie.

Although she was then only in her early twenties, the management of Dale Carnegie & Associates, Inc., was so impressed by her intelligence, enthusiasm and dedication that they offered her the opportunity to be the Israeli sponsor if she would devote two years to training before going back to Israel. She was put through the various courses as a class member, a graduate assistant and trained as an instructor. In addition, she worked in the office of Dale Carnegie Institute in New York, sold enrollments and had frequent in-depth discussions with Carnegie executives. Miss Ailon said: "I probably had more training and more discussions than anybody ever had in the organization because I was there at the right time in the right place. In two years they made me a sponsor."

She arrived in Israel in January 1973 and opened her office. In the beginning it was hard to sell the courses. Because it was a new idea in Israel, people resisted it. Once the first few courses got rolling and word spread that this was a course that really helped people, the program began to attract many students. At first it was given only in English, but after the first four courses, Hebrew became the course language.

Another difficulty was training new instructors. As all instructors must attend a training conference before they can teach, the first instructors had to go to Europe or the United States for these conferences. Later in the year, John McGrath, a senior member of the instruction-training staff went to Tel Aviv to conduct an instructor training conference.

Things went along very well for the first eight months of the Dale Carnegie Course experience in Israel. Miss Ailon decided to go to New York, visit with her parents over the Jewish high holydays and make a triumphant visit to Garden City to receive the accolades of the Dale Carnegie International Headquarters' staff for the success of her work in Israel. However, things did not quite work out that way.

At the convention of the Dale Carnegie organization in San Diego, California, in December 1975, she told what had happened:

"On Yom Kippur, our Day of Atonement, October 6, 1973, I woke up and heard on the radio that war had broken out in Israel. The Arab countries had attacked us. In twenty-four hours I was on a plane back to Israel because that was where I belonged. It was the most scary flight of my life. It was a 747 filled with Israelis going back home. I'm no soldier and behind me were generals and other officers and they were just as scared as I was. We didn't know what to expect.

"Don't ask me what happened during the war. I don't remember. I was in a hospital doing volunteer work; I was busy doing things for my people. The fighting ended, but my world stopped—my Dale Carnegie world. One instructor was in the Sinai as a tank officer; another was a medic somewhere in the Golan Heights—I don't know where. The graduate assistants were in infantry platoons and antitank units—everywhere at the front. The class members and prospects were scattered all over. There wasn't a man around. I was reluctant to phone, because I feared that someone would say: 'Well, they're dead or wounded.'

"Would you believe that for seven whole months there was not one Dale Carnegie class in Israel because there was nobody to run it? I was too depressed. I was so shocked that from a great success I dropped almost to failure. I just couldn't pick myself up. I just didn't have it within me.

"I would sit in the office staring into space. I sat there

waiting for something—for what, I did not know. Then one day the phone rang. It was Yehuda Barkai, a graduate of the second class we gave in Israel.

" 'Dalia,' he said, 'I've just come back.' We made some small talk and somehow he heard in my voice the state of my emotions. 'Dalia,' he said, 'I'm coming over to see you.'

"When he came he asked me if I knew what he had been doing during the war. As he was over fifty, I knew he had not been fighting. He told me: 'I had the worst job of all. I had to notify families that their sons were killed. If I were not a Dale Carnegie graduate I could never have done it. Only the strength I derived from that program kept me from breaking down.

" 'And you were my instructor. What are you doing sitting there brooding? There are people around you who need you. They are depressed, wallowing in negative thinking and just can't get themselves to start working and it's several months since the war ended. You sit here doing nothing. You're a criminal! It's like a doctor who has medicine and someone is dying and he does not give him that medicine.'

"I looked at him as he continued: "Get up! Don't think about yourself. You're the only one in Israel who can teach the Dale Carnegie Course. So get up and get classes going so others can benefit as I did. Only you can do it.'

"I looked up at him and for the first time I began to come out of the shock. 'Get up,' he repeated, 'Stop brooding and start acting.'

"And you know what I did. In a short time I was back promoting and teaching courses, rebuilding my staff, adding instructors and once again bringing Carnegie teaching to Israel.

"That power, that sustained power that brought me back didn't come from me. It came from graduates, the many people who had benefited from my teaching now gave back to me the powers that I had given them.

"All of us, all of us in the Carnegie organization have a power—the ability to teach the Dale Carnegie Course to help other people. We have to give it to them. We owe it to them. And someday some Dale Carnegie graduate will remind you what you possess just in case you happen to forget."

Dalia Ailon Levy's message is carried to people all over the world by hundreds of Carnegie careerists. Over two and one-half million graduates of the courses have benefited from this training. They have gained strength to face life with increased self-confidence and enthusiasm. They have improved in their ability to communicate their ideas more effectively and have gained the satisfaction of enjoying better interpersonal relationships in their business, social and personal lives.

The Dale Carnegie experience does not end with the Course. It permeates the lives of its graduates and keeps working to help them find new paths to more vital, more satisfying and more enriched lives.

Afterword

The Dale Carnegie courses are offered in communities all over the United States and Canada and in fifty countries throughout the world.

If you are interested in learning more about any of the courses, full details can be obtained by writing to:

Dale Carnegie & Associates, Inc.
1475 Franklin Avenue
Garden City, New York 11530

THE DALE CARNEGIE COURSES

The Dale Carnegie Course in Effective Speaking
and Human Relations

The Dale Carnegie Sales Course

The Dale Carnegie Management Seminar

The Dale Carnegie Customer Relations Course

The Dale Carnegie Personnel Development Course